Calculating
Success

Calculating Success

How the New Workplace Analytics
Will Revitalize Your Organization

Carl Hoffmann, Eric Lesser, and Tim Ringo

HARVARD BUSINESS REVIEW PRESS

Boston, Massachusetts

No part of this publication may be reproduced, stored in or introduced into a
retrieval system, or transmitted, in any form, or by any means (electronic, mechanical,
photocopying, recording, or otherwise), without the prior permission of the publisher.
Requests for permission should be directed to permissions@hbsp.harvard.edu, or
mailed to Permissions, Harvard Business School Publishing, 60 Harvard Way, Boston,
Massachusetts 02163.

Library of Congress Cataloging-in-Publication Data

Hoffmann, Carl.

    Calculating success : how the new will revitalize your organization /
Carl Hoffmann, Eric Lesser, Tim Ringo.

       p. cm.

  ISBN 978-1-4221-6639-0 (alk. paper)

  1. Human capital.   2. Personnel management.   3. Employees.   4. Labor
productivity.   5. Organizational effectiveness.   I. Lesser, Eric L.   II. Ringo,
Tim.   III. Title.

  HD4904.7.H64 2012

  658.3—dc23

                                   2011025149

The paper used in this publication meets the requirements of the American
National Standard for Permanence of Paper for Publications and Documents
in Libraries and Archives Z39.48-1992.

From Carl:

I would like to particularly thank my wife Kathleen, whose support in all things as well as the research and writing has been invaluable, and Hank and Arianna, who always provided an anchor for what life really is about.

From Eric:

Thanks to my wife Leah and my daughters Victoria and Eliana—they knew this was important to me.

From Tim:

Thank you to my wife Jenny and son Alexander for their years of patience and support for my constant globetrotting in service to many and varied clients. It is good to finally be home.

[CONTENTS]

CONTENTS

CHAPTER ONE

Applying Analytics to Your Workforce

Realizing Returns on Your Most Valuable Asset

"Business leaders . . . need more rigorous, logical, and principles-based frameworks for understanding the connections between human capital and organizational success."

—Wayne Cascio and John Boudreau, *Investing in People: Financial Impact of Human Resource Initiatives*

The connective tissue between vision and action is analytics. No matter how brilliant a company's strategic vision, it must be evaluated against how well the market will embrace it, how its supply chain can obtain the needed resources, and how much the company can invest in that strategy. Even then, the strategy will fail unless it is clear how to *organize and motivate* the workforce to take action. As obvious as it seems, companies regularly neglect the fact that whenever change is required, they must consider the impact on the workforce and calibrate it to match the new requirements. Key market successes such as Google's ability to exploit search capability, Toyota's principles of manufacturing, and Apple's ability to innovate all required not only a detailed understanding of the business opportunity, but vital knowledge of how to build an organization and workforce capable of executing their vision.

Having built sophisticated analytical models, finance, supply chain, and marketing have long come to the table with dependable business metrics, presenting valuable information about actual and potential costs and profits that form the basis for critical business decisions. But organizations have struggled for years to develop equivalent models and methods that connect organization and workforce measures directly to company performance. As an example, fifteen years ago, David Norton and Robert Kaplan, in their book *The Balanced Scorecard*, noted:

> *[W]hen it comes to specific measures concerning employee skills, strategic information availability and organizational alignment, companies devote virtually no effort for measuring either outcomes or the drivers of these capabilities. This gap is disappointing, since one of the most important goals for adopting the scorecard measurement and management framework is to promote the growth of individual and organizational capabilities.*[1]

We see workforce analytics as a set of quantitative approaches that answer a simple, yet often overlooked question: what do we *need to know* about our organization and workforce to run the company more effectively, and (perhaps most importantly) how do we turn that knowledge into action? These approaches range from a very basic understanding of employee costs to complex models that dynamically balance the supply and demand for workers across multiple time periods and locations. They can focus on short-term outcomes by asking how to better align and motivate workers to achieve the current business strategy. Analytics can also be directed toward a longer horizon, asking what changes in the workforce and its management will be required to achieve future competitive advantage.

Workforce analytics moves beyond the narrow boundaries of the HR function and builds robust strategic and operational models by adding reliable information about workers and the organizational structure to financial, operational, and market data. Companies employ workforce analysis to anticipate what the new organization will look like, what it will cost, and the investment required to get there. Analysis synthesizes an array of facts to design the organizations and jobs of the future, build effective means of supplying the talent to fill those organizations, and understand how to integrate and mobilize workers across geographies and cultures. With such information, executives have the ability to make data-driven decisions based on a clear business case and construct a road map to success.

What Is the New Approach to Workforce Analytics?

Having worked with clients who have wrestled with these issues for the last three decades, we have identified four critical areas where organizations can focus their time, energy, and resources to more effectively use analytics to improve workforce productivity and capability:

- Based on the organization's strategy, *what is the work that needs to be done, and are the processes, structures, and roles designed to efficiently and effectively accomplish it?*

This analytic approach shifts the focus of executives away from simply reducing head count and costs to understanding how an organization can become more productive and competitive—knowing where to invest in their organization and workforce and what the benefits of these investments will be.

- *Is the human capital supply chain filling those roles with people capable of doing the work at the quantity, quality, and cost required of the business model?* This question moves the focus of workforce decisions away from the cost of hiring, training, and developing workers to one that addresses how best to meet the demand for labor required to execute the strategy of the company.

- Once in place, *is the workforce fully engaged and motivated to meet or exceed performance standards?* This analytic approach migrates from quick and narrowly defined performance management fixes to ask a broader but basic business question: what do we expect from our workers and what do we need to provide them to meet those expectations?

- Finally, since change is ubiquitous, *how can we detect the need for change, test innovations in the organization and workforce, and disseminate those throughout the organization?* This approach focuses on understanding how organizations and people can share insights and innovations that allow them to be more productive, while reducing the risks of poorly designed or executed change.

The answers to these questions will have a profound effect on the competitive success of an organization. However, obtaining the answers to these questions requires applying the scientific method, coupled with sound financial analysis and operational realities. The combination of methods allows an organization to translate the findings of the research into profitable action.

Analytics is most successful when applied to an immediate and pressing business problem whose solution is critical to competitive success. The analytical process, therefore, must be done quickly and expertly, often with imperfect data. Throughout the book, we will demonstrate the application of a six-step common-sense approach to addressing workforce challenges. The first four steps focus on understanding *what* has to be done, while the last two focus on turning that knowledge into *action*.

1. *Understanding the central problem.* Too often, executives mistake the symptoms for the disease and act before they fully take stock of the problem.

2. *Applying a conceptual model.* A conceptual model lists the potential causes and solutions of the problem. When combined with business and operational constraints, it can be used to form a hypothesis about the cost and benefits of solutions.

3. *Using the conceptual model to focus data collection* and limit the temptation to boil the ocean. The conceptual model informs what data is critical and what is merely nice to have.

4. *Analyzing the data* to illuminate the causes and potential answers to the challenges the organization is facing, with a focus on defining solutions that stakeholders can reliably execute.

5. *Presenting the findings to stakeholders* to confirm the feasibility of the solution and develop a road map to successful action.

6. *Enabling the solution so the organization can take effective action.* This step almost always requires changes in processes, organization, and people. Defining these changes and providing a road map to implement them are crucial to successfully realizing the full benefit of the analysis.

Understanding the Impact of Workforce Analytics

We hope what we are advocating is intuitive. Know what work needs to be done and how to structure it; provide the right types of people to do it; motivate them to engage in that work; and constantly explore innovations in how that work gets done. But in the rush of daily events, organizations often forget these simple truths. Even when they spend a great deal of time and money analyzing what needs to be done, they forget to consider how the workforce can accomplish it. Next is a cautionary example of such a situation.

*The Oil Field Foreman: Cowboy Hero or
Critical Management Role?*

A few years ago, an oil company found that its returns on investment significantly trailed its competitors'. After extensive analysis, directed by the head of finance, the company calculated ways to improve the bottom line by over $300 million a year: $180 million would come from increased operational efficiency, $70 million from savings in purchasing, and the rest from cost cutting in administration and IT.

To achieve its operating efficiency goals, the company focused on oil field production as the area with highest potential payoff. The company went through a rigorous process to identify the factors that were driving costs and inhibiting production. It built a series of data warehouses that integrated data from finance, production, human resources, health and safety, and environmental systems, as well as external benchmarks, and created, built, and distributed dashboards and scorecards for achieving these new metrics.

One role that was critical to achieving these targets was that of the oil field foreman, the leader of the crews charged with maintaining oil field production and the pumps and pipes that support production. The company gave the foremen a set of scorecard measures that spelled out various goals for production levels, preventative maintenance, personnel costs, training, and safety compliance and told them to control these factors to minimize costs and maximize production. The company frequently changed these targets in response to the price of oil. Furthermore, the effort required to meet one measure often conflicted with another—meeting preventative maintenance schedules and training requirements often meant giving the workers overtime, which increased personnel costs.

Prior to this new initiative, the foremen had gone to work and addressed whatever the day presented. They might have detailed their workers to ride a circuit and check on the pumps and pipelines, or reacted to breakdowns or spills. Their work started over breakfast in a diner discussing the day's assignments and ended in a bar dealing with the day's successes or failures. The new balanced scorecard completely refocused the job of the oil field foremen—what they monitored, how they scheduled activities, and how they managed their workers. Rather than deciding how to handle the workload that was immediate and obvious to them, they were expected to anticipate and balance many competing needs based on mathematically derived relationships. Even the field teams' travel routes and schedules were determined mathematically. The new scorecards based on scheduling and risk algorithms often made no sense to the foremen or the crews.

Their frustration with this new way of working was quick and predictable. They wondered, "What idiot created this mess?" Within several months, the scorecard effort lost support and died without the company realizing the full intended benefit.

Why the failure? The effort started out with all the right ingredients. It had executive support and enterprisewide buy-in, and it could have been a distinctive competitive tool. It was supported with very sophisticated technology that made visible not only the outcomes the company sought, but the factors that could affect those outcomes. The collision of this analysis-based scorecard with the reality of the field foremen's position illustrates the pitfalls encountered when companies don't stop to analyze both sides of the strategy-workforce equation. While the company had calculated what work needed to be accomplished, it spent little analytical effort on determining the *resulting impact* of these changes on the foremen and their crews.

A genuine commitment to the scorecard would have required a fundamental examination of the foreman's role and associated skill requirements. Implementing these new parameters required that foremen shift from experience- and intuition-based decision making focused on their immediate circumstances to information-based decisions that made trade-offs over a longer horizon. This was a critical capability for which they had no background, knowledge, or experience. Unfortunately, management did not appreciate this situation until the clash between numbers and people occurred.

While management recognized the need to train foremen to use the scorecard and explain the measures for holding people accountable, it failed to anticipate the changes required to connect the workforce to the strategy, including:

- *What is the work that needs to be done?* The foreman position became a much more complex and challenging job than previously. It required a significant change in the foremen's personality traits, knowledge, skills, and abilities, as well as the composition of their team and reporting relationships.

- *Is the human capital supply chain filling those roles with people capable of doing the work?* Based on the new demands of the scorecard, the pool of people capable, willing, and interested in doing the foreman job would change. This, in turn, would change the supply chain required to find and develop successful foremen. The cost of acquiring and retaining foremen with the required skills would also increase.

- *Is the workforce fully engaged and motivated to meet or exceed performance standards?* The motivating factors to excel in the job would change. The old foreman position was suited to a kind of cowboy or hero persona that provided substantial intrinsic rewards based on collegiality, friendships, and respect. The role changed from reliance on "in the saddle" experience and intuition to one that relied on data, reports, analysis, and scheduling.

- *How can we detect the need for change, test innovations in the organization and workforce, and disseminate those throughout the organization?* The company could have identified, modeled, and tested all of these changes that affected the role of the oil foremen either through simulations or experiments comparing the viability of different approaches for structuring the jobs and motivating incumbents to perform at their highest levels. The appropriate tools and information to support the new role would have become clear.

Without an analytical approach to understanding and taking action to enable the oil field workforce, the elegant strategy withered on the vine and the anticipated $180 million generated by production efficiencies never materialized.

Why Is This So Difficult?

It is ironic that, as human beings, one of our greatest gifts is our ability to anticipate and to build models that help us understand and take advantage of the future. Yet, we tend not to apply this gift to the most human part of the organization: the workforce. Why do most companies have trouble making the investment in this area when for years, authors have been chastising them for not aligning themselves and their people with strategic and operational needs.[2] We believe that the reason for this persistent and troubling condition has the following root causes, which this book is designed to address.

First, many executives don't appreciate the competitive advantage that they can achieve through their workforce. Too often, they see their employees as a cost of doing business that they need to control and a common denominator that all their competitors must deal with. We argue that this overarching focus on cost management is often shortsighted and misplaced. The cases we cite all added millions, tens of millions, or hundreds of millions of dollars to the bottom line through developing better organizations or improving tools to manage their workforces. The cost of doing the analysis and the amount of time required were small, especially compared to the magnitude of the benefit. Other companies have a cultural bias against adopting a disciplined analytics approach to people, believing people are not inanimate parts. The examples we use in this book show sensitivity to the needs of the workforce by trying to understand the underlying drivers of what motivates workers and how changes in the work environment can lead to increased productivity and profitability. Some executives have been rewarded for relying on their intuition and have confidence that they know their workforce. In fact, as we see in the tale of the oil field foremen, merely defining new metrics, no matter how well thought out, will fail without an analytical approach.

Second, many executives often see getting access to the needed information as too difficult and time consuming. CEOs want immediate solutions and seek to avoid "analysis paralysis." Meaningful analysis almost always requires the integration of data from financial, operational, sales, and human resource systems, all set up to support their separate owners, functional silos, and administrative processes. Each function worries about the security of the data and how it will be used; often each system has different definitions of common concepts and different levels of quality and refresh cycles. This pattern of data ownership and system silos makes quick, as well as continuous, integration of data challenging. We will demonstrate that organizational and workforce analytics can overcome these barriers by quickly building a compelling business case for the investment in the technology and organization that are required to produce, maintain, disseminate, and use meaningful and actionable information. It can transform an organization into one whose decisions are information based and analytically driven.

The third reason organizations fail to use analytics to compete using their structure and workforce is that they don't have a model or simple paradigm that informs how they can use analytics to compete. In fact, there is a general sense that analytics is simply measurement: head count, labor costs, turnover, and so on. One of the questions people ask us most is, "Which workforce metrics are most important?" as if there were a universal truth that all organizations could follow. This is not the case. We believe that workforce analytics is *not* about:

- Counting "heads," but rather knowing how "heads" can be organized and utilized most effectively.

- Reporting "turnover," but rather understanding what skills are being lost, what skills are most valuable, and how to retain those that are essential.

- Building a "catalog" of employee knowledge, skills, and abilities, but rather identifying sets of competencies that managers can use to rapidly select and deploy capable workers at the right time, cost, and place to achieve critical business outcomes.

- Reporting "engagement scores," but rather understanding which aspects of employee satisfaction may lead to high performance and what can be done to improve them.

- Buying "analytic software" and looking for a way to use it, but rather being attuned to the workforce issues that interfere with company success and then adopting the processes and tools necessary to implement the right solution.

Workforce analytics involves modeling the behavior of the organization and the workforce to understand what drives performance within particular needs and constraints. It then informs what tools and processes the organization should put in place to achieve its highest potential. Throughout this book, we will demonstrate how companies are using our six-step method to improve their performance. Our method is a simple and effective way to identify the root causes of a misaligned workforce and strategy. It is a rigorous and systematic approach to understanding the challenges an organization faces in defining and testing successful solutions. Finally, analytics is most successful when applied to an immediate and pressing business problem whose solution is critical to competitive success. The analytical process, therefore, must be done quickly and expertly, often with imperfect data.

As we saw in the previous case, the oil company failed to apply an analytic approach to understanding the changing role of the oil foreman and thus placed a major strategic initiative at risk. However, another company's experience illustrates how to avoid these problems by more effectively diagnosing and addressing the requirements of critical jobs.

The Delta Pilot: Equipment Operator or Skilled Professional?

Delta Air Lines was facing intense competitive pressure to drive down costs while also dealing with a potential shortage of well-qualified pilots. Low-cost carriers were changing the landscape, offering reduced fares and putting pressure on operating costs. Additional strain came as the supply of military-trained pilots, which had always constituted Delta's hiring pool, was shrinking. At the same time, the expansion of multiple cargo carriers and regional airlines meant that the demand for pilots was outstripping the supply and forcing many airlines to accept less qualified pilots. Hiring less experienced pilots required airlines to invest much more in pilot training, management, and administrative support. Many in the industry were promoting the view that cockpit automation and narrowly defined procedures had turned the role of pilot into that of an equipment operator, which no longer required costly and highly trained professionals. Given these pressures, Delta was compelled to consider its options for future pilot hiring.

Delta's flight operations executives believed that changes in the industry were demanding more, not less qualified pilots. In their view, cockpit automation was making flight safer, but not easier. Automation was increasing the cognitive demands of the pilots and altering the division of labor in the cockpit. Industry research pointed to the need for more collaboration, which made the command structure less autocratic. In addition, the entry-level position of flight engineer was being phased out. This meant that newly hired pilots would not have time to learn commercial aviation from the "backseat" but would be expected to immediately operate at a high level of expertise. Increased air traffic and changes in the air traffic control systems were also putting new demands on the job. Changes in how planes were scheduled and the staffing at the airports increased the intensity and variability of operations.

Delta thought of its pilots as decision makers and leaders who played a critical role in optimizing the company's performance. Delta had traditionally hired pilots with highly skilled military backgrounds and was very selective, turning down one in three applicants with this experience. Its pilot population was composed of exceedingly motivated and well-trained recruits who could quickly master complex equipment and procedures. Delta believed it had the advantage of an engaged professional group who assumed responsibility for the safety, comfort, and efficiency of flights. The quality of its workforce allowed for an enviably lean and efficient management structure. If the capabilities of the new hires were diminished, flight operations would face substantial restructuring and investment, as the costs of training, administration, and daily operations were projected to increase dramatically to compensate for a less experienced and prepared pilot workforce.

The importance of building an effective pilot supply chain was consistently reinforced in interviews with highly rated, experienced Delta captains. Overall, their comments could be summarized in one phrase, "Don't make my job any harder than it is by changing the ability and attitude of the guy I am sitting next to in the cockpit!" It was clear that accepting less qualified pilots or those who did not share Delta's cockpit culture could mean extensive and costly changes to cockpit management, as well as increased risk to flight safety.

Addressing the problem

Delta executives decided that the least expensive and most effective way to deal with the cost pressures of the changed candidate pool was to improve the pilot-selection process to ensure bringing in pilots with "the right stuff." This meant knowing exactly *who* they wanted to hire and *how* to identify these individuals. A variety of government organizations and academic researchers had extensively studied the jobs of military and commercial pilots over the previous sixty years, but Delta needed to know not only what worked in the literature but what characteristics were essential *in its organization*. It needed to know how to obtain pilots best suited to fit its needs from a pool of candidates increasingly trained in civilian programs and recruited from regional carriers with varying qualities of training and standards. To answer this question, Delta turned to analytics to accomplish the following:

1. Explicitly define the behavior and attitudes that make an excellent Delta Air Lines pilot.

2. Understand what knowledge, skills, abilities, and personality traits underlie those behaviors and attitudes.

3. Determine the best ways to measure the underlying attributes; that is, how to capture the best measures from background characteristics and experience, interviews, and selection tests.

4. Define an effective, cost-efficient hiring process that selects candidates with "the right stuff."

Delta began with a disciplined process of job analysis to clearly define the work of the Delta pilot. This process produced a valid, unique, easily communicated set of twelve behavioral objectives for its pilots. Underpinning these behaviors was a set of knowledge, skills, capabilities, and personality traits. Delta then translated these, in turn, into selection tests and evaluation methods that it gave to a sample of current pilots and all new hires. The initial assessments were, based on experience, highly predictive of their performance in training and on the job. The analysis produced a robust model of what made a good pilot at Delta Air Lines.

This analysis process did not just simply focus on short-term results, but studied pilot performance over twelve years. When Delta Air Lines hires a pilot, it is making a thirty-year investment in human capital. Sustained performance over a career is critical to passenger safety and to Delta's success. The analysis identified ways of weeding out pilots who would find it difficult to adapt to the continuous demands of the schedule, training, and travel. Through this process, Delta took out of consideration those pilots who were likely to become disgruntled and disengaged from the demands of flying.

Reaping the benefits

The process of studying the role of a pilot and determining how to select a good one from a heterogeneous and uneven supply required substantial investment, but had significant, measurable benefits. Delta moved from relying almost solely on the military as a source to hiring 50 percent of its pilots with no prior military experience and training. Automating the application review and testing substantially reduced the cost of the selection process. It also greatly decreased the time from the review of the application to hire, putting Delta in a better position to compete for pilots. But most importantly, improved selection reduced training problems by 20 percent, while avoiding costly changes to existing training and providing a more productive workforce. Within a short period of time, these benefits more than paid for Delta's investment in workforce analytics and the changes made to the selection process.

The benefits have also been tangible with respect to the overall effort required to manage the pilot workforce. As Captain Steve Dickson, Delta's senior vice president of flight operations, recently said, "Many of my peers in the industry would love to have the workforce I do. I have the future leaders which they feel that they don't have. My workforce requires less effort to manage in the day-to-day operations; my pilots know what to do, make sound decisions and are professional in their execution."

This process has led Delta to use an analytically based approach to reinforce its management philosophy. It has used the twelve behaviors to understand how cockpit automation requires a better definition of the division of labor for cockpit operations. It has also used the behaviors to focus the role of captain on the critical areas of the job and to construct observational tools to regularly assess pilot performance in the cockpit.

It has also implemented an additional analysis of pilot behavior to develop a probation program and study the nature of flight delays in airport operations.

The Six-Step Analytical Process: The Intersection of Science and Business

Analytical efforts often start small. Typically, a specific business unit faces a critical workforce issue that threatens its ability to accomplish significant business goals. The initial analytical process often provides substantial rewards to the bottom line, frequently in the millions of dollars, and provides a valuable infrastructure that makes the next challenge easier to solve at less risk and cost. The analytical approach is then adapted to subsequent workforce challenges and becomes the standard procedure for understanding human capital issues. The participants also become adept at supporting analytically mandated changes with processes and decision support systems that can be sustained and adapted to new challenges. These new capabilities become as valuable as the initial savings.

There is a discipline that underpins effective workforce analytics. In using the word *discipline*, we are not referring to drill sergeants or after-school detention. We are referring to a structured approach to inquiry that combines good business practice with established scientific method. At first glance, following this disciplined approach to analytics may seem like a lot of work. But, much like developing a good swing in golf, it can become quite natural and have great rewards, often millions of dollars in increased profit. When followed, this discipline greatly reduces the time and risk of doing the analysis poorly and spending a great deal of effort and money for little benefit. The combination of good business practices with the disciplined approach of analytics breathes life into the statistical and mathematical analysis and helps ensure that the numbers connect the people and the business.

Our experience has led us to believe that there are six important steps that companies must follow to understand and solve human capital management challenges, which are summarized in table 1-1.

Step 1: Frame the Central Problem

While it may sound obvious, taking the time to understand the real issues confronting the company is essential. Line managers and executives are very good at recognizing the immediate issues they face and usually eager to take action with the information they have at hand. Unfortunately, they often take those actions without fully understanding the underlying cause or what additional problems might result from their uninformed actions. Asking an executive to slow down and consider other alternatives may be the equivalent of standing in front of a charging bull. However, without setting the immediate issue the company faces in the larger context of the business, any analysis will be focused on confirming an executive's hunch instead of thoroughly examining and solving the problem.

Consider the long-term implications of the workforce decisions made by Circuit City, a U.S. electronics retailer.[3] Facing significant cost pressures in early 2007, it decided to lay off thirty-four hundred of its highest-paid sales personnel, knowing that those cost savings would immediately pump up the bottom line. While this layoff resulted in a one-time cost savings for the company, the loss of its most experienced workers caused further deterioration of its customer service reputation and

TABLE 1-1

The workforce analytics process

Step 1: Frame the central problem.

- Interview key players in line management, HR, finance, operations, and other functions, as indicated, to build perspective.
- Review existing documents that provide context: organizational structure, central business initiatives, project plans, high-level allocations of responsibility.

Step 2: Apply a conceptual model to guide the analysis.

- Identify workforce and business variables that are likely to have associations with the problem outcome.
- Be alert to idiosyncratic events and additional data that could be relevant.

Step 3: Capture relevant data.

- Pursue appropriate data across all relevant business units: HR, operations, finance, marketing.
- Reconcile differences in definitions, codes, and time frames.
- Store valid data in analytical database.

Step 4: Apply analytical methods.

- Employ appropriate formal quantitative techniques, looking for stable patterns over time.
- Examine results and identify robust explanatory models.

Step 5: Present statistical findings to stakeholders.

- Construct presentation of results that is accessible to business managers without a statistical background.
- Validate and enrich statistical patterns with stakeholders' experience through interviews and focus group discussions.
- Identify any new problems that surface and consider the need for further analysis and understanding.

Step 6: Define action steps to implement the solution.

- Operationalize changes in policies, procedures, and management actions designed to produce desired changes in workforce behavior.
- Monitor and document changes in management actions and workforce outcomes.

enabled competitors to cherry-pick its top-performing sales-people. Ultimately, this short-term fix did little to improve Circuit City's long-term viability; it declared bankruptcy in January 2009, with over thirty thousand of the remaining individuals losing their jobs as well. Although Circuit City faced many challenges, if it had focused the question on how to achieve long-term sustainability of the business through a more effective workforce, the results may have been different.

The nature of the business and the manner in which a company chooses to compete in the market are critical to framing the analytical questions. This goes beyond the fiscal constraints placed on possible solutions to include the fundamental identity of the company: how it has succeeded in the past and how it envisions competing in the future. A company must undertake analytics through objective lenses, based on facts that paint the reality of its markets and competitive position. The possible solutions must factor in the company's competitive and management philosophy, as well as its financial and market reality.

Step 2: Apply a Conceptual Model to Guide the Analysis

Those involved in workforce analytics run the risk of becoming lost in the accumulation of data that companies have available, while at the same time finding themselves stymied by the seeming lack of *critical* information. Analysts need a way of determining what data is important and what they can do without, as well as some basis for understanding how missing data may limit the interpretation of their findings. A conceptual model provides the analyst with a framework to identify useful data for addressing the problem at hand, as well as the types of information that should be scrutinized, the kinds of questions that should be posed, and how to interpret the results of the analysis.[4] Adopting models from the behavioral sciences can help determine what information is essential to capture from existing systems and what additional information needs to be collected to study the problem and design a solution.

There are often hundreds of relationships among those variables that "just might" indicate the path to managing the workforce more effectively. There are data-mining tools that offer the ability to quickly explore these relationships and determine their statistical significance. Unfortunately, this blind empirical approach can produce "results" that make no sense and can point companies down the wrong path. While the length of hemlines and the winner of the Super Bowl may be correlated to the performance of the stock market, they are not the basis for sound investment strategy. Similarly, the fact that valuable employees leave to take positions at higher pay may not be a reason to raise the salaries of all high-performing employees. A conceptual model describes the variety of factors that lead employees to look for positions elsewhere and thus will guide analysts through the labyrinth of data relationships, allowing them to question serendipitous results and reject spurious findings.

A well-articulated conceptual model enables executives to understand the research process and comprehend the results in the context of their business model. For example, the analytical database that supported the pilot section analysis at Delta Air Lines had over five hundred variables. The conceptual models Delta adopted from the scientific literature also matched their intuitive understanding of pilot performance and helped focus the analysis on understanding how three fundamental capabilities contributed to pilots' performance at Delta. First, does the candidate have sufficient command of the principle of modern aviation to solve problems quickly? Second, does the candidate have the personality to adapt to the culture of the cockpit and the demands of the job? Third, can the pilot operate under pressure with multiple demands and still function? Finally, how do these factors work in conjunction with one another to create superior performance? This set of simple concepts and questions focused Delta's efforts on measuring these concepts and building predictive models of how they affect pilot performance. Without them, Delta ran the risk of getting lost in a maze of relationships among those five hundred variables.

Step 3: Capture Relevant Data

As mentioned earlier, most companies are rich in data and poor in information. Useful analysis depends on collecting and constructing measures that can be clearly tied to employee productivity and corporate profitability. The necessary information usually resides in different databases that must be integrated, and even then, the data is often not in analyzable form. In the case of Delta Air Lines, the analysts had to combine and reconcile information from eleven different databases, including applicant tracking, testing, training, work histories, performance observations, and flight scheduling.

Analyzing the effect that the workforce has on company success almost always requires the integration of finance, sales, operations, and human resource information, each with its own unique definition of organizational relationships, head count, and costs. This lack of standardization makes simple comparisons difficult. As we will discuss in chapter 7, The Royal Bank of Scotland made a great effort to combine data from human resource systems, operations, and marketing to understand how it could manage workers in its branches more effectively to increase profits. This process involved getting key senior-level executives into a room to agree to share and standardize data. As painful as this effort was, it had great payoff for branch operations.

Step 4: Apply Analytical Methods

Effective workforce analysis must be guided by someone with formal training in mathematics and/or statistics, following disciplined methods of inquiry designed to identify causal links and build valid models. There are many statistical techniques available to perform organizational and workforce analysis, including simple cross-tabulations, regression, stochastic process modeling, factor analysis, cluster analysis, survey research, and experimental design. All have their appropriate applications; all have their strengths and weaknesses. Knowing which to apply to what questions is critical to producing valid findings.

Useful analysis requires an understanding of study effects and uniqueness of the samples, which can produce incidental relationships that are not the basis for valid generalizations.[5] For example, over the last seventeen years, Delta Air Lines has done extensive studies of how pilots' backgrounds predict their performance on the job. In one study, the job performance of pilots with extensive experience in high-performance fighter jets far exceeded the performance of pilots with other backgrounds. Subsequent studies using different samples of pilots never reproduced these results. Hence, the fighter jet criterion would have been misleading to use in a selection process. In contrast, studies consistently found that prior experience in all types of military and civilian jets *was* predictive of good performance at Delta. Avoiding an investment in incidental relationships that are unreliable predictors of outcomes requires research training, experience, and discipline.

Disciplined analysis can also help identify arcane results. In an effort to increase both sales and customer service, a telecommunications company found a seemingly contradictory relationship. Sales were higher in those teams that had longer tenure, but also in teams with high turnover rates. (See chapter 4 for the full explanation of this paradox.) A detailed analysis of this contradiction provided insight into the characteristics of highly effective team leaders and how their efforts could add significantly to sales of services and retention of customers. The process of finding valid and reliable patterns in complex data depends on skilled analysis, as well as the judgment and experience of the analyst, not simply automation.

Step 5: Present Statistical Findings to Stakeholders

Translating the analytical findings into action requires that management can understand and relate to the results presented. Otherwise, it will resist the information and the necessary changes implied. Regression equations, process models, and factor and cluster analyses do not immediately speak to the non statistician. Results must be presented in a way that is con sistent with the management philosophy and vernacular of the company. Engaging stakeholders and inviting dialogue that connects analytical results with business experience are essential. The stakeholders' responses to the presentation of analytical results breathe life into the statistics and enrich the understanding of the data. Such engagement is the key to finding the best solutions and obtaining commitment to transformative actions.

In one life sciences company, an extensive statistical analysis indicated that career progression (characterized by a simple change in job title combined with a yearly pay increase) was a more powerful motivator and retention tool than large pay increases or stock options. Yet, it was not until analysts presented clear graphs that demonstrated the impact of career progression on retention of key personnel that executives embraced the relationship (see chapter 6). Once they clearly saw the results of the analysis, managers actively helped design effective ways of retaining key employees and brought forth other problems that workforce analytics could solve.

Step 6: Define Action Steps to Implement the Solution

Identifying the relationship between particular workforce actions or attributes and company profitability is not enough to accomplish change. The analytical process must translate proposed solutions into a sustainable action set that supports and monitors the desired outcomes. This entails determining what processes and tools will be effective in supporting new actions by managers. The tools often need to be embedded in the managers' existing routine to provide appropriate alerts, content, and actions that are linked to targeted events.

The analysis of the life sciences company showed that the strongest retention tool for key performers was career progression, and that the intervention had to happen at a key point in a worker's career—after the sixth year of employment. To retain key workers, the unit manager needed to target a timely "career conversation" that specifically recognized an employee's value to the company, addressed his or her career aspirations, and conferred a new job title along with the normal pay raise. Simply providing such a directive to unit managers would not be effective, since it would inevitably be lost in the pressures of daily business. Instead, the company developed a set of tools to alert unit heads when their workers were approaching their vesting date and provided information to assist them in assessing the value of the employee and the available career opportunities. This empowered the unit managers to judge what actions were appropriate to retain highly valued employees and how to structure that career conversation. Without these tools, the insights gained from analysis would not have been regularly translated into effective actions.

Workforce Analytics: For Good or Evil?

Analytics is often thought of as a cold, heartless way to manage the workforce. It sometimes makes people fear an Orwellian approach to management and has been compared to using science to raise the stroke count for the slaves on a Roman galley. However, we argue that companies can use workforce analytics to make more justifiable decisions and prevent arbitrary actions that can have a negative impact on individuals. As John Boudreau highlights in his book *Retooling HR*:

> *Is it because people are not widgets, and out of respect for their free will and humanity it's unfair or wrong to use the same logic for workforce decisions as we use for decisions about more inanimate objectives like inventories and machines? No.*
>
> *In fact, it's arguably more unfair and disrespectful to employees and job applicants to make important decisions about where to invest in their development, performance and careers in less rigorous ways than those applied to more traditional resources.[6]*

The value of workforce analytics is that it provides the logical basis on which companies can make difficult decisions. Jeff Joerres, chairman and CEO of ManpowerGroup, the global leader in innovative workforce solutions, understands both the difficulty and criticality of translating strategy into the behaviors of the workforce. No one may be in a better position to appreciate the need for workforce analytics than Joerres, as ManpowerGroup places over four million workers with its clients each year.

He runs a company that values the combination of fact-based analysis and management judgment. Joerres points out the value of having a rigorous process for evaluating management actions against the reality of the workforce:

> *How many times do you hear the general employee population refer to the management team as a bunch of idiots? Sure, the employees can dislike the management team. However, leadership is not based on popularity, but respect for the decisions management makes.*
>
> *Earning that respect requires facts that describe the reality of the company's competitive situation, a clear explanation of what actions need to be taken and why. It requires understanding how that message will be heard and what support will be provided by the company to help the workers make the transition. Analytics can help the management team focus on the reality of what can be done; to see a path through frustrations and emotions.*

Where This Book Will Take You

This first chapter has highlighted a number of ways in which companies can create competitive advantage by gaining insight and acting on the structure and behavior of their workforces. Chapters 2 through 5 will examine in depth how particular companies are using analytics to address a number of common workforce-related challenges. Chapter 2 shows how analytics can link strategy and organization design. Chapter 3 highlights the analytical approaches that companies use to build effective human capital supply chains to fill the positions in their organizations with the right people, at the right time and cost.

Chapter 4 demonstrates how companies use analytics to ensure that once workers are in place, they are focused and engaged in meeting the objectives of the company. Chapter 5 examines how innovations are identified, tested, and shared across the organization.

Chapter 6 will provide a capstone case example of an IT organization that was able to apply an analytic approach to retaining key individuals, illustrating a number of different analyses and outcomes. It demonstrates how solving a simple problem can lead to greater insight and action. Finally, in chapter 7, we will examine in detail the different technologies, processes, organization structures, and staffing that are required to successfully develop and sustain an analytical culture.

CHAPTER TWO

Translating Strategy into Profitable Action

"An organization's vision and competitive strategy is the battle plan for moving into the future and achieving its goals . . . It is the marching orders for the subsumed business units, divisions, departments, functional areas, teams, and individuals to follow as they maneuver on the battlefield of business."

—Jeffery Schippmann, *Strategic Job Modeling*

T he connection between mission, strategy, organizational structure, and staffing is starkly demonstrated in the transformation of the U.S. Armed Forces over the last decade. This was captured succinctly in an article by Andrew J. Bacevich in *The Atlantic*:

In the 1990s, the Powell Doctrine, with its emphasis on overwhelming force, assumed that future American wars would be brief, decisive, and infrequent. According to the emerging Petraeus Doctrine, the Army (like it or not) is entering an era in which armed conflict will be protracted, ambiguous, and continuous—with the application of force becoming a lesser part of the soldier's repertoire.[1]

The shift in mission from destroying large-scale enemy forces and infrastructure to surgically weeding out small insurgent groups from the communities they infest has been significant. Its impact has extended from how troops are organized and deployed down to the individual roles within combat units. In an attempt to avoid civilian causalities and collateral damage, there has been a movement away from the use of tanks, artillery, and large-scale air support and toward a greater reliance on small units using discreet force and precisely targeted technology. Units are composed not only of well-trained combat teams, but also of individuals focused on government affairs and rebuilding civilian infrastructure. While these areas of expertise have always existed in the army, their relative importance, the timing of their involvement, and their integration within combat units has substantially changed. The capabilities required of the combatant have also changed to include sensitivity to the local language, culture, and politics of the environment in which they work.

The U.S. Army is clearly not the only organization facing these challenges. New competitive threats, changing demands of the marketplace, technological innovation, and shifting demographics are all placing pressure on companies across a wide swath of industries. Yet, many lack the frameworks and processes necessary to translate strategy into workforce action. Before you can build a talent pipeline to provide the right people at the right time and cost, and then motivate them to do the right job, you have to define what the right job is and have in place the appropriate processes, organization, and technology to support the individuals performing that job.

Establishing an analytic approach to aligning business strategy and workforce performance provides two important benefits. First, it builds a solid foundation for decision making, ensuring that the organization has an evidence-based platform on which to make trade-offs between alternatives. But, equally as important, it can serve as a catalyst for action. By providing leaders with the ability to describe the seriousness of their competitive challenges and the insights to overcoming these challenges, analytics provides a call for action and a road map for change. These tools are urgently needed to overcome the natural inertia and resistance to change found in most organizations.

For this chapter, we use some case examples to illustrate how analytics can translate strategy into workforce action. We start by looking at how Qantas Airlines used scorecard analytics in a unique way to articulate the goals of its *strategy*, frame its strategic alternatives, and drive change throughout the organization. We then examine how a business unit in a global manufacturing firm used analytics to design the changes in processes required of its new *operational model.* The third example explores how a community college used job analytic techniques to align its organization and *define work* to provide better and more economical service to its students and community. Finally, we show how Luxottica and IBM translated the capabilities required for key positions into *standards* for recruiting, selecting, and deploying workers and forming the backbone for developing an effective human capital supply chain.

Each of these examples deals with marshaling information that forces people to see the challenges of their existing business models and to think of new ways of acting. Each case uses the six steps we outlined in the first chapter:

- Frame the central problem.

- Apply a conceptual model to guide the analysis.

- Capture relevant data.

- Apply analytical methods.

- Present statistical findings to stakeholders.

- Define action steps to implement the solution.

The Challenge of Organizations: Translating Strategy into Action

As we saw in the case of the oilfield foremen, the cascading of strategic measures down through the organization is only one step in achieving the objectives of the corporation. Changes in processes, organizations, technology, and workers are necessary to translate these goals into actions. This transformation from strategy to action takes place in four different areas, captured in figure 2-1.

- *Developing the business strategy.* The business strategy represents the starting point for any discussion about the workforce. Decisions on markets, customer segments, target revenues, margins, and allocations of costs frame the basic issues about the role that human capital plays in the success of the firm. The business strategy, in many situations, cascades down the organization through a number of metrics, which are often aggregated and communicated via the use of a scorecard. The scorecard, as Robert Kaplan and David Norton describe, is a collection of balanced aspirations; goals that, if achieved, will provide a sustainable business model "that highlight[s] those processes that are most critical for achieving breakthrough performance for customers and shareholders," and reflects the envelope in which the organization must operate.[2]

- *Creating the operational model.* From the strategy, an organization needs an operating model to translate its goals and targets into a blueprint that each of the business units

FIGURE 2-1

The four areas of organizational analysis

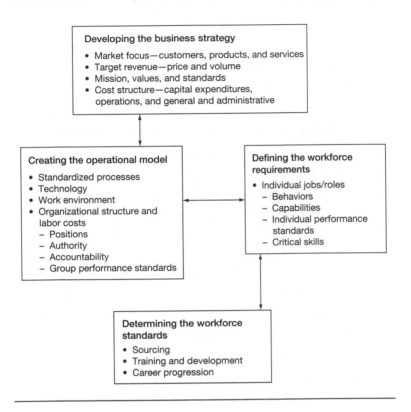

Developing the business strategy
- Market focus—customers, products, and services
- Target revenue—price and volume
- Mission, values, and standards
- Cost structure—capital expenditures, operations, and general and administrative

Creating the operational model
- Standardized processes
- Technology
- Work environment
- Organizational structure and labor costs
  - Positions
  - Authority
  - Accountability
  - Group performance standards

Defining the workforce requirements
- Individual jobs/roles
  - Behaviors
  - Capabilities
  - Individual performance standards
  - Critical skills

Determining the workforce standards
- Sourcing
- Training and development
- Career progression

can execute. The blueprint includes business processes, organizational structure, productivity standards, and enabling technologies. The interaction among these dimensions determines the needed skills and capabilities required for success.

- *Defining the workforce requirements.* New processes require new jobs and roles that facilitate the execution of those processes. As part of the definition of these new positions, a company must define accountabilities, rewards, and reporting relationships to clearly illustrate how employees will actually execute the work and support the company's goals.

- *Determining the workforce standards.* Finally, a company needs to establish standards to determine whether workers possess the capabilities required to fill those roles. These standards must support recruiting, selecting, developing, and rewarding workers. This last step is critical in supplying the specifications—the bill of materials—for the talent supply chain we discuss in the next chapter.

In theory, integrating these areas should be simple and easy. Know what business you are in and how you will attack it. Build efficient processes and an effective organization to execute that strategy. Create roles and an environment within the organization where workers can succeed. Establish reliable ways of identifying and developing workers who will succeed, and develop reliable measures of performance so they can monitor their success. In each area, demonstrate how efforts to improve the organization and workforce capabilities will improve the company's performance.

These are concepts every good manager should know, but linking the manager's actions to these four analytical areas to create a high-performing organization is hard because they are often thought of, and acted on, separately. This is what we observed in the case of the oilfield foreman position. Coordination across each level is difficult because each area of analysis has a different owner and a different initial starting point, and is supported by different information systems geared toward different objectives, using different data. Often, basic concepts do not have common definitions across functions or the systems that support them. For example, minor differences in the definitions of a department, the cost of a worker, direct versus indirect labor, what an employee is, and how to count workers make sharing data, undertaking analysis, and discussing the results quite difficult.

Developing the Business Strategy

At its best, strategy defines not only the goals of the organization, but also the guidelines that it must adhere to in order to achieve those goals. Strategy targets results, that is, market penetration, sales, and profitability, while articulating what the company must do to achieve those results—the operational costs of labor, materials, advertising, investments, and money. It also articulates the financial, labor market, and environmental constraints that affect the ability of the company to execute its strategy. Often, the components are captured in scorecard metrics that make these parameters explicit. These metrics are too often considered a fixed reality, a straitjacket on operations instead of the articulation of a dynamic system that can be managed in a variety of ways to achieve the desired results. Analytics can set up a creative dynamic where effective management of the organization and workforce can become an important tool in achieving the company's overall strategy.

Driving and Measuring Change at Qantas

In the early part of the past decade, Qantas Airlines realized its competitive position was threatened by low-cost carriers. The organization had only been privatized a few years earlier, and the culture was still very much one of a government-run entity where workers felt protected and entitled. Typical of the airline industry, it had challenging labor relations issues. Qantas's cost basis was too high, especially labor costs, which were driven by generous salaries, pay raises, leave policies, and high training costs. Its pay and benefits set the standard for Australia, so any action the company took to control costs would be very public and closely watched by all the unions and employers in Australia.

Frame the central problem

Qantas's strategy was to create new business models and reengineer existing models, while simultaneously pursuing labor-cost reductions. At the same time, Qantas needed to change the attitudes and behaviors of both management and twenty different labor groups. Fact-based analysis played a key role on both fronts. Analytics highlighted issues that executives did not want to confront, but at the same time, it provided guidance to individuals in solving those problems. The analysis also became integral to negotiating with the unions, developing bargaining positions, and relating information to investors and the public.

Apply a conceptual model to guide the analysis

At the center of this analytics-led transformation was Kevin Brown, the head of human resources. His goal was to motivate the business unit heads to anticipate an intense competitive environment and take action. Key to his success was adopting a unique scorecard approach. After trying a number of approaches, he chose to focus on one critical metric—unit labor cost per available seat kilometer (ASK), which combined elements of both labor costs and output. Business unit heads could be held accountable for achieving their transformation by controlling the components of this metric:

- *Total manpower costs*—by managing head count and/or the rates of pay for those heads or outsourcing work to lower-cost providers.

- *Cost drivers*—by eliminating or reducing the amount of nonvalue-added work or redundant work that drove the need for workers.

- *Productivity*—by affecting processes through business process redesign, automation, and/or improving the capabilities of workers.

Whatever action a business unit chose to implement, it had to lead to an overall reduction in the ASK metric. Focusing on this composite measure and its components solved the problem that had vexed previous improvement efforts: the presence of many separate and competing measures such as head count, labor rates, productivity measures, customer satisfaction, and quality. Many separate indicators had allowed business unit heads to choose their favorite, often self-serving measures for improving their individual unit's performance measures without addressing the larger organization's need to become competitive.

Capture relevant data

To track the transformation, Qantas needed rapid and clear information to support each unit's analysis and decision making, as well as to monitor progress and hold unit heads accountable. It developed a scorecard containing standard metrics that, taken together, determined the three critical components of unit labor costs per ASK that Qantas thought would achieve the goals for each business unit:

- Full-time equivalents—total hours worked divided by standard workweek.

- Manpower cost for the business unit—for each labor group including contractors and outsourced work.

- Drivers—the amount of work the business unit accomplished specific to its function.

- Productivity—the amount of work accomplished per full-time employee.

- Unit cost—manpower cost divided by the relevant drivers.

Qantas asked each business unit to model how it would effectively manage its contribution to ASK. This task required obtaining, cleaning, and integrating data from many administrative systems within the company: finance and operations, as well as HR. It required validation of the information with the business unit heads, determining standard and consistent definitions of simple concepts such as "full-time equivalent" and "department" as well as developing measures of productivity for baggage handling, cargo, catering, aircraft maintenance, and passenger service. Obtaining reliable and accurate data from HR, payroll, finance, and operational systems was a challenge since each system had been designed to support the separate business function. For example, the data to determine how many bags were loaded in a day and how many hours baggage handlers were required to work on that day came from two different systems that were not designed to be integrated. Brown and his team decided that the data did not have to be perfect; it had to be good enough. They ignored errors in the data that were not material to the results.

Apply analytical methods and present statistical findings to stakeholders

Once Qantas determined the data was as valid as possible, HR worked with the business unit heads to understand the magnitude of the problem they were facing and explore trade-offs with regard to restructuring the work, outsourcing or offshoring, and using contingent workforces. Everyone understood from the beginning that this transformation would require time and development through many stages. At each stage in the transformation, models were constructed to measure and test the possible cost or benefit of changes and demonstrate to executives how they could control costs while maintaining or increasing services. Determining the cause of inefficiencies and how they could be alleviated while lowering the risk of labor action and customer dissatisfaction was hard work. In many cases, business units and labor unions claimed "special circumstances." Inefficiencies in baggage handling could come from weather, airport congestion, delays in the network, and equipment problems, all out of the control of airport services. Consequently, Qantas spent a great deal of effort coming up with valid, reliable, and controllable actions and measures for which each business unit would be held accountable.

Define action steps to implement the solution

Qantas used analytics to define the problem the business units were dealing with, understand and test alternative solutions, and involve the managers in interpreting the analysis and examining solutions. What would changes in work rules mean in terms of cost reduction and service? What was the cost or benefit of locating crews in foreign domiciles? The results of these analyses suggested the need for radical changes to all parts of the airline: redistributing the lines of authority and accountability, redefining the intensity of the work and how it got done, how it was measured, and the qualifications and capabilities of workers presently in the company and of those the new organization would need.

Analyzing these multifaceted problems led to a variety of solutions, such as how and where to establish offshore bases, how to make sourcing decisions, and where and when to use contingent employees. Qantas's call and service centers became driven by sophisticated scheduling algorithms that matched workers and their skills to customer demand. Stochastic models determined the future supply of pilots and remedied the projected shortfalls in supply. Each year, analyses put workforce plans in place to meet the competitive needs of the company. Qantas translated these into metrics that held managers accountable for achievement and became part of determining their compensation.

Brown knew that the transformation would be disruptive, especially in the Australian labor environment. Data-based facts gave him and the executives a way through the transformation. The impact on the make-up of the workforce was huge. In nine years, Qantas separated 7,000 workers and offered another 19,000 voluntary severance packages, averaging more than 2,500 workers per year moving out of the business. Simultaneously, Qantas hired over 32,000 workers into the newly transformed organization over this period. Ultimately, Qantas reduced ASK per unit labor costs by 10 percent, but also increased route miles by 75 percent and revenue by 60 percent, becoming one of the most profitable airlines in the world. Analytics successfully guided this transition and helped avoid many of the potential catastrophes that acting without data could have caused. As Brown said, "Many times in this transition we had to change our game plan in midstream—data and analytics gave the executive team the capacity to weigh options and explain our actions to the stockholders, workers and the press."

Creating the Operational Model

The values of the company, its objectives, and resource allocations are set at the corporate level. As we just saw with Qantas, these translate into goals and metrics, often in scorecard format, that cascade down for the business units to implement. The business strategy is then realized by organizing the workforce and technology into processes designed to profitably execute that strategy. Analytics play a critical role at the formation of the operational blueprint.

Techniques such as process modeling can help define what, when, and how work will be accomplished. Business process modeling helps to clarify what activities to eliminate, simplify, support through technology and automation, or consolidate. It spells out the dependencies and information required to support the activities and decisions at each step of the process. Information technology is playing an increased role in this effort. Using modern systems to capture this information can greatly speed the development of the software and systems required to rapidly implement new processes. With the support of these tools, business analysts are becoming known as business architects, with the power to redefine the fundamental components and processes of many business units. But the results of these efforts and the activities they design still need to be combined into roles that workers can perform. These roles must in turn be aggregated into an organization structure that broadly defines the matrix of positions that are required to accomplish the work, the accountabilities of each position, and the reporting structures required to monitor and support the processes being accomplished.

A focus on processes is particularly applicable to manufacturing and supply chain functions that are driven by highly predictable flows of work and connected by routine chains of action. The processes need to reflect the volume and quality of the work, as well as be capable of accomplishing that work within the cost allocated for that process. Process design also highlights the conditions and circumstances under which work will be accomplished, for example, how teams will work globally, virtually across time zones, cultures, and languages.

Analysis of the financial, organizational, and reporting structure of the company must also accompany a process analysis and
subsequent redesign. In his recent book, *Collaboration,* Morten
Hansen provides a compelling example of how Apple's organization structure promoted innovation, while Sony's organization
inhibited it.[3] The inefficiencies that confronted Sony are en-
demic to many large organizations. Silos are reinforced by division of labor, budgeting, and accountabilities assigned to
different components of line organizations. The powerful terri-
torial boundaries thus created require compelling analysis to
break down. As companies become more horizontally aligned to
be responsive to their customers, they need to consider the limitations of their existing organization structure to establish the
business case for change and build the new design, processes,
roles, and staffing levels of a new organization.

Redesigning Work at ABC

As the magnitude of the changing competitive landscape cascades down to each business unit, decision makers confront the
stark reality of meeting a company's strategy. In the next case,
about a U.S. manufacturing plant, we highlight how changes in
processes have a significant impact on the design and composition of the workforce.

Frame the central problem

The general manager of an American manufacturing plant
(ABC) was confronted with the reality of how to translate the
strategic objectives of his company into the actions of his workers. Falling margins and high costs jeopardized the future of the
plant. After visiting many similar plants throughout Asia and
Europe, he found that some were achieving much greater

efficiency through the application of horizontal processes and technology that were more responsive to market demands. He also observed that staffing in these organizations was leaner and job roles were broader. How could he take the plant from its traditional vertical processes, represented in figure 2-2, to the more desirable horizontal structure he was seeing in other plants, represented in figure 2-3?

Apply a conceptual model to guide the analysis

The realignment around horizontal processes would require a transformation of the organization and the workforce's capabilities. This new paradigm required the commitment of the entire plant management. The general manager needed to translate his vision into terms that would motivate his organization to change. He would have to illustrate current inefficiencies and make new processes seem advantageous and achievable. He needed analytics to clearly describe the goal and provide a road

FIGURE 2-2

Vertical processing at ABC

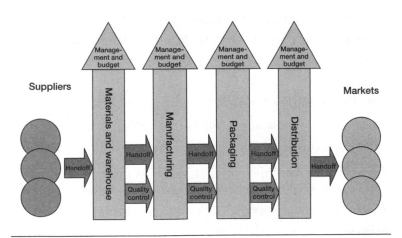

FIGURE 2-3

Horizontal, customer-driven flow at ABC

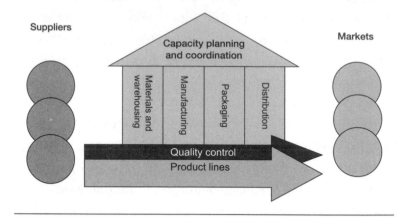

map that would mobilize his workforce to give up a familiar set of concepts and behaviors and adopt an unfamiliar paradigm.

Capture relevant data and involve key stakeholders in the analysis

The next step in accomplishing the metamorphosis began by quickly assembling measures for all the company's process and costs, and identifying where and why bottlenecks and inefficiencies were occurring. Benchmark data collected from similar facilities indicated that ABC's manufacturing costs were much higher than similar U.S. firms and two to three times greater than the best-in-class manufacturing plants located in Europe. This fact was encouraging, for it meant that a manufacturing plant in a highly regulated and unionized environment could potentially compete with the cheaper labor in Asia.

ABC collected data on staffing levels, pay, role descriptions, and reporting relationships. It conducted activity-based surveys to establish the time spent and importance of those activities to its success. From simple descriptive statistics, it found that the plant was top-heavy and had too many layers of management. As is often true for top-heavy organizations, activity-based analysis indicated that managers spent less than half their time managing their teams and instead were focused on responding to requests for information and coordinating across silos and on special assignments. Further analysis of the activity-based data showed that frontline workers spent less than half their time on manufacturing and about the same amount of time troubleshooting, looking for information, and waiting for instructions.

ABC conducted focus groups with hourly workers and management in each of the divisions to flesh out the statistics with qualitative information on their experience of daily work with regard to time allocation, scheduling issues, communication, management practices, work requirements, and work group interaction. From these discussions, it found that communication was top-down; frontline workers were not empowered to make decisions and, in many cases, not invited to share their ideas. Frontline workers had few opportunities for cross-utilization, because silos and budgeting reinforced the managers' views that they owned the workers and that any work done outside their function was at a cost to them and with no benefit to them. Finally, coordination across the manufacturing process was poor, resulting in surpluses and shortages of intermediate products up and down the production line.

Apply analytical methods and present statistical findings to stakeholders

The combination of qualitative and quantitative analysis was necessary to capture the attention of management and point out the magnitude of the inefficiencies and dysfunction. ABC was now prepared to rethink the new processes. It made the decision to adopt a customer-driven, continuous flow of product through the plant. In its new model, the factory would create only what the end customer purchased. ABC would use technology to provide visibility up and down the line so demand signals could be as real-time as possible. While this situation might appear as a classic case of process reengineering, what differentiated ABC's approach to the change was its focus on modifying the workforce requirements needed to make this change truly successful. This focus involved using the activity-based survey results to determine:

- What work to eliminate.

- What work to automate.

- How the company could reassign and consolidate the remaining activities into fewer positions aligned with the process.

- What changes in authority and responsibilities the remaining positions would have.

- What capabilities those new positions required.

- What performance measures, rates of pay, and rewards would attract, motivate, and retain workers with these capabilities.

- Who in the existing workforce could perform those roles and have those responsibilities and what additional training they would need.

ABC ran optimization models with various assumptions about the volume and timing of work to test the capacity of the new business and organizational model to produce the needed volumes of product at the required cost. It fleshed out the new model with projected process flows, roles and capabilities, staffing levels, costs, and savings, which indicated a strongly positive financial return. The benefits associated with this change took the form of better inventory control, increased product quality, and customer satisfaction, as well as reduced head count and total labor costs. The new operating model required a much flatter organizational structure, thinning out midlevel management as daily decision making was pushed down to the shop floor. The old vertical silos would be transformed from operational business units to resource pools of equipment and people, optimized to meet the production needs of the market. This meant adopting a collaborative matrix approach to management that would replace the old top-down structure. New roles for managers, supervisors, and frontline workers were carefully defined by required behaviors, responsibilities, and performance levels, with accompanying metrics.

Not only did the new roles require that employees have deeper and broader skills, but also *fundamentally different personality traits*. Frontline workers would no longer simply operate machines, but would be empowered to highlight plant conditions, anticipate problems, and assist line supervisors with planning. Successful workers in these roles would be attuned to multitasking and find satisfaction in work that was variable and flexible, rather than unchanging routines. They would also have to be comfortable with more independence and taking more initiative. First-line supervisors would be transformed from command-and-control positions within their function to key roles in integrating activities and communicating across functional areas to identify production opportunities and forestall problems. While the number of workers would decrease greatly, their value to the organization and their associated rate of pay would need to increase. Overall, this increase was minor compared to the overall benefit.

Define action steps to implement the solution

The next step was to conduct a gap analysis to determine how future needs matched up with current talent. We will describe this very simple form of workforce planning more fully in chapter 3. ABC analyzed data to determine how many incumbents had, or could acquire, the necessary capabilities that were appropriate for the new roles, how many it would terminate, and how many new hires it needed. The processes and steps in this analysis are summarized in table 2-1.

TABLE 2-1

Example of transition plan for functional units							
Functional group	**Present workforce head count and costs by function, based on reporting**	**Transition steps: Human resource capacity plan**					**Future workforce head count and costs by function, based on analysis**
		Head count loss		Remaining workers capable and interested in performing the new roles	**Head count gain**		
		Expected amount of normal attrition	Expected number of workers who will be unable to perform the new roles		Expected number of new hires	Expected number of workers needing training	
Materials and warehouse							
Manufacturing							
Packaging							
Quality control							
Engineering and maintenance							

ABC estimated that about 30 to 40 percent of the employees would be a poor fit with the new model. The costs of dismissing employees who no longer fit, hiring new workers with better skills, and training incumbents and new hires were specified and included in the financial analysis.

ABC used the data from the new model and the gap analysis to produce a human resource capacity plan that laid out the necessary steps to accomplish the transition over a twelve-month period, specifying the sequencing of technology implementation, investment, and movement into new roles. The plan also detailed periodic initiatives and quarterly milestones designed to overcome the inertia of the old structure and reinforce positive change with the new business model. At the end of the process, ABC had achieved the objectives of the plant redesign. It had reduced head count by 25 percent and labor cost by 20 percent and greatly increased overall throughput of the plant.

Defining the Workforce Requirements

As we saw in the previous section, process modeling helps define new, more efficient processes and the roles that support them. This approach to defining work identifies the tasks to eliminate, automate, and/or capture in workflow to control critical processes and finally define the activities that the workers must execute. Process modeling is a very valuable tool for highly routine processes that have predictable sequences of action.

At the same time, there are many industries that are not as tidy as manufacturing or large, high-volume administrative functions such as claims processing. Government services, sales, research and development, consulting, and many large-scale construction and systems integration projects are characterized by highly variable work driven by reacting to direct contact with the customer or the environment, or dealing with ambiguous competing needs. These organizations must take a different approach to analyze and redesign work. One approach, job analysis, is a quick and efficient way for companies to understand what they are paying their workers to do and how to make that work more efficient.

Developing New Competencies at a Community College

The next case illustrates how one organization used the principles of job analysis to quickly understand the impact associated with a shift in strategy, unscramble the confusion that the shift caused, and rapidly improve service while decreasing costs.

Frame the central problem

To enable closer contact with the community and become more responsive to its customer base, the administration of a large community college (CC) was decentralized and distributed among its four main campuses. Each campus served a different student demographic as well as different local employers that would be hiring students over the next several years. Subsequent to the change, the administration felt that while the separate campuses were more responsive to the students, the process of delivering those services was inefficient, costly, incomplete, and chaotic. Rather than decomposing all the various processes that support the college, the administration undertook a comprehensive survey and job analysis to address inefficiencies and improve service delivery. By identifying activities that were critical to achieving the community college's objectives and redefining the jobs required to accomplish these activities, the college hoped to reduce the amount of complexity and redundancy within the organization.

Apply a conceptual model to guide the analysis

CC conducted an activity survey that asked nonacademic staff to identify which tasks they were engaged in, how much time they spent on those activities, and how important they perceived that activity to be to CC's success. Since the analysis was intended to result in a better alignment of CC from top to bottom, it included all levels of the organization, from the chancellor to the maintenance staff. This survey also asked respondents to identify the capabilities (the knowledge, skills, abilities, and personality traits) required to perform their jobs. Each worker's response was then linked to his or her total compensation. This analysis provided the following information:

- *The actual level of effort and cost of labor that CC was spending on each set of activities required to meet its goals.* CC then compared this to the budgeted costs allocated for these activities as well as its stated strategy.

- *Duplicative efforts, inefficiently designed jobs, and activities that were being neglected.* Based on this, the organization could be rationalized, staffing levels adjusted, and budgets better allocated to strategic objectives.

- *An analysis of how capabilities clustered or grouped* was fundamental to developing an efficient human capital supply chain and providing:
  - The link between compensation and sets of capabilities to understand the internal and external equity of the compensation policy, thus improving the retention, mobility, and deployment of workers.
  - The link between capabilities and selection methods to make a more efficient recruitment and selection process.

- The career paths and development activities to allow workers more control over their careers and provide for CC's future needs.

- A common definition of the capabilities of workers to facilitate sharing of resources across the four campuses.

Capture relevant data

The starting point for the survey was to compile a single, nonredundant list of activities from all existing job descriptions for the more than five hundred noninstructional job titles. During this review, CC found that no standard job descriptions existed at the college. Jobs with similar titles could look very different based on their description, and jobs with very different titles could share many of the same activities. In some cases, there were no job descriptions at all.

The activities in the job descriptions were standardized, producing more than nine hundred distinct activities. Clearly, workers filling out a questionnaire with over nine hundred activities would view it as torture and not take it seriously. The survey had to be more focused and targeted to specific occupation groups. Analysis of how these activities were shared across jobs revealed eighteen distinct job families.

CC asked focus groups, composed of subject matter experts (SMEs) within each of the families, to review each list of activities, delete or add activities not listed, and finally validate and edit the activities. At the same time, it asked the focus groups to identify the knowledge, skills, abilities, and personality traits (KSAPs) required to perform these activities. Analysts consolidated the activities and standardized a list of more than three hundred KSAPs that were applicable to one or more of the eighteen job families. The results of this analysis produced a definite, clear, limited, and nonredundant set of activities and capabilities within each job family. CC collected surveys from approximately 90 percent of all noninstructional employees, providing more than adequate representation for studying jobs at the community college.

Apply analytical methods and present statistical findings to stakeholders

As anticipated, the surveys revealed a large number of tasks endorsed by incumbents that seemed not to be a part of their jobs. Many jobs had forty or fifty activities, confirming the fear that workers' efforts were scattered and inefficient. This type of analysis commonly reveals that many workers are not focused on "playing their position" or even aware of what their position is. The results offer surprises. In this case, one campus president and two secretaries had the same response patterns. In another example, maintenance assistants, maintenance specialists, and the supervisor of building and grounds clustered together, indicating that there was no clear definition of supervisory roles.

CC held feedback sessions to confirm these and other findings. Information gathered from the sessions also helped shed light on how the actions of leadership led to the results and how to fix the problems. The analysis and focus groups showed that workers had taken to heart the message to be responsive to their customers—to such a degree that their efforts were interfering with the operations of the college. Many people in different positions were spending much of their time actively engaged in advising or at least talking to students about academic courses, career choices, financial aid, and other matters that were not a part of their jobs. This was especially troubling because the college had implemented a Web site, a service center, and an automated registration process to reduce this effort. While the most visible customers—the students—were getting disproportionate service, the needs of the larger community and surrounding businesses were being ignored. The survey and discussions with representatives of the community showed that activities associated with marketing, community outreach, and contact with local industry were not occurring to the degree anticipated.

While workers included many activities that went far beyond their intended work, the patterns of their response proved very useful in redefining their roles. Cluster analysis of survey response patterns revealed that there were ultimately only eighty-nine distinct jobs—many fewer than the initial five hundred or more jobs the community college had identified. Ultimately, the analysis showed that CC could eliminate up to eighty positions, because the work could be done more effectively through existing automation or reorganized into more efficient roles. For instance, supporting counselors with an additional clerical position helped free up 50 percent of the counselors' time. The number of counselors could be reduced, while the remainder could be more effective in dealing with the students' academic and financial needs. More effective counselors and better use of the portal and service center could reduce the need for departmental clerical staff to deal with students' ad hoc inquiries. As work became more efficient overall, service levels increased, while the total number of workers decreased, even with the addition of new jobs to handle marketing and community and business outreach.

CC also discovered that one key set of activities in marketing was being completely ignored. Little time and focus was spent on understanding the labor market needs of the communities CC's campuses served and developing courses that would allow industries in the surrounding areas to meet their future labor needs. As a result, CC defined new jobs to reach out to the local business and labor markets to understand and better fill their unique needs.

CC used the results of the survey and analysis to develop new job descriptions that included six to twelve activity statements per job. This meant eliminating activities, aggregating those that were too narrowly defined, and adding new activities that were important to the success of the new strategy, but not currently being performed. These new activities stressed not only the immediate responsibilities of the work, but also the division of labor and the coordination required to deliver excellent service. Overall, CC was in a better position to serve the communities, industries, and students that made up its market and, at the same time, control costs.

Developing Workforce Standards

The final step in defining work is providing the tools to assess whether someone possesses the capabilities to succeed in his or her job. How can a manager know that the candidate has what it takes to perform well? How can a manager look at an employee's performance and be effective in coaching that worker on how to improve? These necessary tools ensure that the inventory of workers meets the capabilities and standards (the bill of materials in supply chain terms) required to fill the positions in the organization. This bill of materials focuses managers and workers on the work that they need to accomplish. In this section, we will describe how analytics connects the selection and deployment of workers to improved performance.

We present two cases that illustrate different ways that companies have used analytics to build the inventory of workers with the quality required to execute their strategy. The first focuses on the need to establish a model for identifying candidates from outside the organization. For industries such as retail and hospitality that hire many individuals on a continual basis, the ability to screen out those who will not be adequate matches for positions can save significant recruiting expense, reduce overall turnover, and increase productivity once they begin to perform their jobs. The second case highlights the challenges associated with the internal deployment and movement of individuals to roles within the organization. As more organizations move toward a project-based environment, the need to quickly and successfully match those with available skills to projects becomes an increasingly important competency. Underlying this capability is a common definition of the skills and attributes that can be transferable across projects or lines of business. Establishing common hiring models and skill taxonomies are both critical requirements to building the talent supply chain, which we discuss in the next chapter.

Selling Sunglasses at Luxottica

Luxottica Retail is one of the leading eyewear retailers in the world, operating more than sixty-two hundred stores under the well-known brands Pearle Vision Centers and Lenscrafters in North America and OPSM and Laubman & Pank in the Asia-Pacific region. One of Luxottica's brands, Sunglass Hut, faced significant workforce turnover, with almost 100 percent of its associates leaving every year. While such high levels of turnover are often considered a cost of doing business in the retail industry, Robin Wilson, the senior director for workforce analytics at Luxottica Retail, knew that reducing this number could have a direct impact on the business in terms of both reducing hiring costs and improving store productivity and sales. Her analysis found that 70 percent of turnover was occurring within the first three months. This suggested that something within Luxottica's recruitment and selection processes was amiss. Working with her finance team to identify the direct and indirect costs associated with this level of turnover, Wilson identified several million dollars of opportunity that the company could regain.

Sunglass Hut had adopted the hiring practices used by Luxottica's other brands, which relied on three core competencies linked to selection criteria. The competencies focused on sales ability, conscientiousness, and customer service. These applied to all Luxottica brands. However, there were key differences in how work was done within a Sunglass Hut store compared to other stores. Sunglass Hut locations tended to be smaller stores or kiosks, with only one or two employees working within the store at any given time. Further, the stores tended to attract shoppers who were much more likely to purchase on impulse, rather than those purchasing corrective lenses, which tends to be a planned decision.

Given these factors, Wilson worked to develop a new set of capabilities that directly addressed the specific conditions that sales personnel would face within a Sunglass Hut. She designed an experiment to test whether hiring workers with these competencies would increase sales. She screened a test group of candidates using new interview questions and compared them to a control group that received only the standard screening questions. Wilson found a statistically significant difference in the turnover and the amount of time it took for new salespeople to reach their expected quotas, favoring the new selection process. After reviewing the results of the tests with line management, Sunglass Hut revamped its screening protocols, introduced new competencies into its recruiting process, and saw notable reductions in turnover and time to productivity for new sales associates. Further, having seen the impact of this recruitment and turnover analysis, other brands within Luxottica also began to reexamine their applicant-screening processes and found they too were able to improve productivity and reduce turnover through screening tools that were more tailored to their business models.

Building a Common Expertise Platform at IBM

The previous case dealt with how one company used analytics to better recruit and hire people from outside the organization. But most companies fill openings from within. They look to reduce the risk of a new hire by drawing on existing staff that have the knowledge, skills, and familiarity with the culture to succeed. Unfortunately, companies often find filling positions internally more difficult than hiring from the external labor market. Even as economic and market forces are demanding a more responsive and flexible workforce, companies face inefficiencies within their internal labor market. These inefficiencies include available pools of labor trapped within organizational or geographic silos as well as the need for trusted standards that accurately described the capabilities and costs of workers to quickly match and assign them to open positions.

In the early part of this decade, IBM faced just these challenges. Analysis showed that the company was often seeking to reduce certain skills from one unit while another unit was seeking to grow these same skills. Delays in finding available workers to staff client projects were contributing to lost revenue and client dissatisfaction. Finally, IBM was looking for ways to broadcast project needs to their global workforce to provide growth opportunities for top talent. Getting control over these forces would save many millions of operating costs, grow revenue opportunities, and simultaneously increase profit and preserve talent within the organization.

To fill positions quickly and build teams that often spanned the globe, managers had to trust that they were filling positions on their projects with people who could do the job at the productivity level and cost that they could afford. Similarly, workers had to trust that, if selected, they could succeed at the job, grow their capabilities, and enhance their careers. Key to this effort was developing a single global taxonomy of capabilities that would define the capabilities of workers anywhere in the organization and in any location around the world.[4] This taxonomy would enable IBM to more effectively assemble project teams and drive higher levels of workforce utilization.

A great deal of effort went into analyzing the standard roles in organizations and project teams. The capabilities that supported these roles were defined by dimensions that corresponded to the family of roles common to IBM's work, for example, project management, process consulting, IT architecture, and so on. Each dimension had a number of levels of proficiency that defined the responsibility, scope, and expertise of a worker. To obtain certification that a worker could operate at a level of proficiency, he would have to be observed by their project managers and immediate supervisors demonstrating that he had successfully exhibited that capability. For instance, in the project management category, workers would be rated on how many phases of projects they supervised, the size of the teams and budget they managed, their ability to track progress and hold people accountable, and their ability to communicate with the client and identify and resolve issues. Analysis provided each level with clearly defined, unambiguous, and observable behaviors. This certification process became part of the annual performance review process, but supporting data gathered throughout the year became a part of the daily conversation between employees and managers as they served their clients.

This taxonomy has enabled a more efficient internal labor market, which, in turn, has driven increases in utilization, client responsiveness, decreased cost, and increased retention of top performing workers.

Conclusion

Each of the cases in this chapter represents how companies can use analytics to make the link between strategy and the human capital required to execute it. Using the ASK metric, Qantas focused its entire organization on rethinking how work was done in each business unit. ABC used analytics to challenge the traditional vertical organization of its manufacturing plant and eliminate needless levels, while defining the new organization and roles that would be required to succeed in reducing costs and increasing productivity. The community college used analytics to realign its workforce to more effectively meet the needs of the students and communities it served. Finally, Luxottica and IBM, by articulating the standards required by their organizations, found ways of more effectively and efficiently staffing positions and increasing their profitability and responsiveness to their customers.

As demonstrated by the examples in the chapter, there are a range of analytic approaches that can help organizations define and execute their business strategy. Developing an overarching set of workforce targets and metrics as part of the business strategy can help define the potential opportunities for improvement, as well as provide managers with the insights to target their change efforts. Process modeling can identify opportunities, needed skills, and capabilities and redeploy resources toward value-added activities. Job analysis can help determine whether people are actually performing the roles and responsibilities needed to execute the strategy, as well as highlight areas of overlap and omission. The development of selection models and expertise taxonomies enables managers to make more effective choices regarding the resources that are needed to ultimately perform the work. Each of these analytic techniques, by themselves, provides a greater window into the development of a productive workforce. However, the techniques are best used in conjunction to give executives and business architects the line of sight they need to improve organizational performance.

Highly effective and efficient organizations have developed creative ways to rethink work and the analytical techniques to model and test their ideas. A company's competitive strength lies in how it organizes its workers to use state-of-the-art technology to control its competitive and resource environment. This is the key to competition in a global marketplace. In one form or another, we've heard executives comment: "Hiring smarter workers to do the same dumb work will not make us more competitive no matter how much more we pay them. But working smarter will make us more competitive." Having discussed what companies are doing to work smarter, we now turn to what companies are doing to build their talent supply chain to fill positions and how they apply analytics to predict the demand for workers, manage their supply, and allocate and deploy those workers to their most effective use.

CHAPTER THREE

Balancing Talent Supply and Demand

"If we could just build a system to identify the people we have and utilize them better, it would lower costs associated with laying off people from one group while hiring that same talent into another. It would limit project delays and increase revenue."

—Chief Information Officer for a large aerospace and defense company

In 2002, IBM set out on a mission to transform itself into a more services-based organization to capture growing demand for consulting services along with its hardware and software offerings.[1] In July of that year, IBM purchased PricewaterhouseCoopers' consulting arm for an estimated $3.5 billion. Having added 30,000 services professionals to its workforce, IBM instantly catapulted itself into one of the largest providers of consulting services in the world. The move was roundly praised in the business press; however, the immediate focus turned to how IBM would assimilate and make productive (and profitable) such a massive workforce of highly educated knowledge workers.

From the start, it was clear that the task to match global supply and demand for a consulting services workforce and connect these services to IBM's hardware and software business would be monumental. To meet the challenge, in 2003, IBM launched its workforce management initiative (WMI)—a highly innovative and effective approach to mapping global supply and demand for IBM professionals. WMI combined software and effective workforce analytics to provide a framework for aligning the systems, policies, capacity management, and deployment processes, with the technical architecture needed to increase talent effectiveness on a global scale. The result was a significant improvement in IBM's ability to get the right people with the right skills to the right work in a timely manner. With the impetus and acquisition of a large professional services workforce, IBM used this innovative approach to workforce analytics to solve the problem of balancing talent supply and demand on a truly global scale, to better serve its clients.

In the previous chapter, we focused on the business model, defining the positions needed to execute the model and identifying the relevant skills and capabilities needed to fill those positions. This framework represents the realization of a company's strategy and how it will organize and manage its workers to meet the demands of its customers. This chapter describes how to ensure that workers occupy positions where and when they are needed, and at the right cost.

Filling those positions is not as simple as it may appear. As the types of work and the volume of activities change, the demand for workers will change as well. Depending on the industry, the need for workers can occur hourly or take place over many months. In retail, travel, and leisure, the flow and demand of customers change hourly as well as seasonally. In the

pharmaceutical, electronic, aerospace, and automotive industries, companies must fulfill demand for workers as a response
to immediate customer needs and to product life cycles that
may take decades from R&D to market.

At the same time, the supply of workers needed to fill these
positions is constantly varying. Incumbents either leave or
move to other jobs within the company. Further, the capability
of the existing workers to handle the volume of work constantly
changes due to a variety of factors, including employee experience, motivation, and technology. Externally, the aging workforce threatens the availability of skilled workers, while the
broadband revolution has increased the access to talented individuals around the globe. Understanding and acting on the
ongoing changes in both internal and external labor markets has
become increasingly more challenging and complex.

This chapter outlines the analytical efforts that companies are
making to understand the dynamics that drive the demand for,
and the supply of, labor and to ensure the workers are in place
where and when they are needed. There are a number of analytic
activities that are the subject of this chapter, represented in
figure 3-1. They are divided into planning and execution:

- Planning

  - *Projecting the demand forecast* for workers with needed
    capabilities. A company can combine scenario plan-
    ning models of the projected demand for the goods and
    services that company will sell, derived from the annual
    planning process, with the organization and staffing
    models developed in chapter 2 to estimate how many
    workers it will need and when.

  - *Determining the supply forecast* of workers to fill these
    roles. A company can run statistical process models to

FIGURE 3-1

Building an on-demand talent supply chain

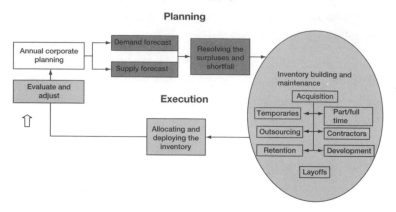

project the supply of the existing workforce that will be capable of doing that work.

– *Identifying and resolving the gaps between demand and supply* to build an inventory of workers. Combining the outcomes of these two analyses will expose where the company may have too many or too few workers with the necessary skills and costs. Linear programming and optimization techniques can be key to dealing with these shortfalls and surpluses. Should the company transfer and train existing surplus workers to fill shortfalls or lay off those surplus workers and acquire new workers through hiring or the use of contractors? Each choice has its own costs, benefits, risks, and time lines.

• Execution

– *Building and maintaining the inventory* of workers to meet the needs of the company. Once a company has analyzed these factors to produce the best solution, it can set in motion a human resource capacity plan to build and maintain the needed inventory of workers. The company must track and analyze execution against this plan to ensure that necessary workers will be available to the line managers who need them.

- *Allocating and deploying the inventory* where and when it is needed. Next, analytics is key to developing the systems that will allocate those workers to where and when they are most needed and best used. This might be a labor-scheduling algorithm for a retail store and/or a labor exchange for a global services firm.

- *Evaluating and adjusting.* Finally, a company should constantly evaluate the effectiveness of these efforts to ensure that the workforce is effectively contributing to the company's results. Is the human resource capacity plan delivering the needed workforce? If not, why? What can be done to improve it?

The supply chain analogy does, however, have limits. Recently, a great deal has been written on the need for, and importance of, balancing talent supply and demand. Leading experts and organizations, such as Peter Cappelli at the Wharton School, have explored the concept of a "human capital supply chain," in which capabilities are made available when the need arises.[2] This analogy is helpful because it points out the rigor and tools that are required when companies recruit, select, develop, and deploy their employees. However, we also believe that organizations sometimes take an overtly simplistic view of the complexities and interdependencies inherent in developing an "on demand" workforce. People are not widgets; they cannot be comprehensively described within a "bill of materials" or an "ingredient list." Individuals come with a set of distinctive skills, preferences, and requirements that motivate them to achieve well beyond their "specifications" or that hinder achievement of their potential. Their attributes are mutable; workers can be inspired and taught, and their needs and interests change over time as they go through their careers, all causing potential variability in their performance. Workers have a life cycle that is more complicated to model than a machine part. Workers can also choose where, and for whom, they want to work, an option not necessary to consider when addressing the sourcing and transportation of raw materials. Given these differences, organizations should be wary of claims that they can manage the supply and demand for talent with the same precision as other commodities.

The outline of this chapter follows our six-step approach. It frames the problem of building a talent supply in the context of the competitive position and strategy of the company as well as the global and market forces that company must respond to. It provides the key components of a conceptual model that can guide the necessary thinking and analysis to match the number of workers with the appropriate level of work and how to address mismatches between the two. The chapter also highlights the data required to perform the analysis, and the tools necessary to make the projections and understand and act on the trade-offs and decisions. Critical to the success of building a talent supply chain is managing the cultural and organizational change required to enable companies to take advantage of these workforce management capabilities. For instance, an important question that companies are facing is how analytics will affect the management of critical roles. Will first-line managers be reduced to simply administering what is proscribed by these systems or will their role be expanded to proactively use the information provided by these systems to respond quickly to the demands of their markets and workers?

Frame the Central Problem

One imperative is that organizations understand the context for analysis. The results of the analytics we describe in this chapter need to be interpreted in light of the three key factors:

- What business objectives influence the optimal size of an inventory of workers?

- What time horizon does a company need to address?

- What is the geographic distribution of the workforce?

What Business Objectives Influence the Optimal Size of an Inventory of Workers?

Finding the optimal level of employees requires understanding the organization's basis for competition within an industry. The decision to compete on different dimensions, such as price, quality, and customer experience, has direct implications for the overall size of the inventory of needed workers and how they are deployed. The relative importance of four business goals will have a direct impact on how organizations consider the size of their talent inventory:

- *Cost reduction.* For many companies that we have worked with, the primary benefit they seek from human capital supply-chain improvements is to reduce labor costs. The savings include the ability to more accurately match actual labor usage to labor forecasts, which can, in turn, reduce unnecessary hiring, overtime expenses, and the use of agencies and outsourcing providers. For instance, Covenant Health Systems, a nonprofit, integrated health delivery system with three thousand employees, has seen significant cost-reduction benefits through improved labor scheduling.[3] It used workforce analysis that was part of its employee-scheduling system to fully integrate with its time and attendance application, and provide real-time data availability on staffing levels. By scheduling health-care professionals, including nurses, operating room technicians, respiratory and physical therapists, and ER paramedics, Covenant balanced the cost of overstaffing with the risk of having appropriate resources unavailable when needed and improved overtime management. Covenant achieved a 145 percent return on investment. It also avoided the use of staffing agencies and reduced the amount of time that patient-care managers spent on staffing activities by fifteen hours per month.

- *Customer satisfaction and revenue enhancement.* Many service firms—such as retailers—are focusing on revenue enhancement, in addition to cost reduction, as a driver for improving labor planning and scheduling practices. By more accurately matching staffing levels and their capabilities to customer demand, these companies are expecting sales personnel to more rapidly answer customer queries, work with customers to appropriately match products with their requirements, and make suggestions for additional products that customers might need. Retailer Metro Cash and Carry (a European wholesale grocery business) upgraded its labor-scheduling and forecasting processes as well as simultaneously implemented new labor-scheduling software. The result was a 50 percent reduction in checkout wait times (along with a decrease in labor cost of between 3 percent and 7 percent).[4]

In addition, for those companies involved in higher margin, lower transaction businesses, increasing the overall availability of staff with greater knowledge of products and services is an important way for labor scheduling to contribute to improved customer satisfaction. Cost savings can also be achieved indirectly; reducing the amount of administrative time managers spend on creating schedules would allow them to devote more time to either working directly with customers or training employees on selling techniques.

- *Employee satisfaction.* Improvements in labor deployment and scheduling can also be beneficial in increasing employees' satisfaction, which in turn can raise their engagement and productivity. Using self-service tools, employees can more easily provide input about the number of hours and shifts they want to work, which can be incorporated into the optimization of the work schedules. Staff members can also obtain access to upcoming schedules, request time off, and offer to take on additional hours as needed, while factoring in their capabilities and limitations. Pilots and flight attendants regularly use this capability to satisfy their personal and family needs, while meeting the demanding schedule requirements of the airlines. As a consequence, when they come to work, they are not preoccupied with distractions that would interfere with the focus and execution of their work. Adding worker preferences to the scheduling algorithm produces schedules that workers are able to fulfill and lessens the absenteeism and turnover and associated poor customer service and low productivity. In addition, when technology facilitates consistent application of scheduling rules, employees are more confident that their schedules accurately reflect negotiated agreements and that their paychecks are driven by the actual time and schedules worked.

- *Increased managerial control and responsiveness.* As the pace and complexity of business increases, managers struggle to respond to unexpected changes in demand and operational practices. Labor planning and scheduling software solutions provide a better understanding of future workloads and staff, serving as a platform for managers to measure operational performance, formulate contingency plans, and wrestle with trade-offs and difficult decisions. For example, catalog retailer L.L.Bean has leveraged computerized software tools and mathematical models to improve management's ability to plan its labor force and schedule its call-center agents. Major initiatives have included improved workload forecasting and economic valuation of incremental investments in labor.[5]

  Another area where labor scheduling can play an important role is in compliance management. As John Anderson, a director with Kronos Incorporated, a major provider of workforce management software indicates, "When you are dealing with large numbers of employees distributed across many locations, an automated process for scheduling staff, tracking hours worked, and managing absence can prevent the company from running into compliance problems with both employees and the government."

Balancing risk and optimizing productivity require companies to understand the implications across all of these different dimensions. If the company is too cost conscious, it may risk having workers unavailable to service customers or produce goods. This would potentially translate into lost sales and market opportunity. If the company is focused solely on meeting customer demands, it may require more workers to be available or to work at times and hours that exceed their ability, driving up overtime pay and/or increasing absenteeism and turnover. Effective use of supply-and-demand information requires management discretion. Managers need to respond to conditions on the ground and not be driven blindly by numbers. Clearly, even within the same industry, the resolution of these issues will be different based on the business model and management philosophy. A high-end specialty retailer would have very different requirements and trade-offs compared to a big-box store. The former would tend to slightly overstaff and risk higher costs because it competes on service, while the later would tend to understaff, knowing it can risk poor service because its customers want low-cost goods. Similarly, a consulting firm focused on strategic consulting would have a different view of how to staff engagements and the needed inventory of workers compared to a full-service IT implementation shop.

What Time Horizon Does a Company Need to Address?

Every industry wants the right person in the right place at the right time and cost, but the rhythm, impact, and costs associated with making a mistake vary greatly. The time and cost required to fill positions also has a profound impact on the analysis and choice companies face. If an operating room technician, pilot, or member of a construction crew fails to show up for work, the consequences can be costly in money, damage, and reputation. On the other hand, if a retail or customer service clerk fails to show up, the immediate damage is low, but repeated occurrences may do substantial harm to the productivity, reputation, and sales of the company. There are significant differences in finding, developing, and replacing highly skilled professionals compared with retail and customer service workers. Both the cost of an error and the time horizon for planning all affect the analysis and actions companies must take.

In industries such as retail, health care, travel and transportation, hospitality, telecommunications, and, increasingly, manufacturing, the ability to allocate and reposition employees daily or even hourly can have a direct impact on organizational productivity, customer satisfaction, and growth. Advances in technology often involving real-time tracking of workers, their current availability, and costs have made it easier for organizations to take more analytic approaches to deploying and allocating resources so that they can make better, more informed decisions over increasingly smaller increments of time. A retail store manager may face the happy occurrence of having more customers in the store than she expected, but be confronted with a very real cost decision. Does she ask someone to stay beyond his shift and incur overtime or call someone in and deal with the lapse in service until the person arrives?

For other companies, the time horizon of matching individuals to work occurs over a period of weeks, months, or even years. This is particularly true in organizations whose business models are based on large project delivery and rely on highly skilled and tightly integrated teams. This includes professional services firms, contract research organizations, electronics companies, life sciences firms, and aerospace and defense contractors. These firms often require unique skills and capabilities that require years to develop. The capabilities are critical to a project's success but may only be brought to bear during specific and discrete times during the project life cycle.

In certain industries, balancing labor supply and demand requires an even longer-term horizon for making workforce decisions. For some companies, the time from identifying potential candidates to the time they are able to work for the organization can be measured in years. People who need certification and credentialing, such as nurses, nuclear power plant operators, pilots, and electrical lineman, can require years of course work and apprenticeships that may or may not involve specific firm investments. Therefore, organizations need to take a long-term view that addresses what they perceive to be the internal demand for labor, as well as the larger business and demographic trends that influence talent supply.

What Is the Geographic Distribution of the Workforce?

In the age of globalization, knowledge workers, and virtual teams, the physical location of workers is becoming less relevant. Ironically, being freed of this constraint brings new challenges. As many companies shift from being based locally to more global approaches to staffing projects, managing the inventory of talent and the deployment of assets becomes more difficult. They must develop tools to evaluate the capabilities of individuals, identify their availability and associated costs, and make trade-offs across the projects that may compete for their services. This information, supported by decision support tools, becomes critical in determining project success and company profitability. For example, a project manager looking to staff individuals on an IT project may wish to understand a number of factors, such as:

- Can a less experienced software developer who costs $50 per hour in one country and who may be less productive substitute for a more experienced developer who costs $100 per hour, if the less experienced individual will be available to work on the project three weeks earlier?

- Is there a constraint in the number of software-testing personnel in one location that requires the use of outside subcontractors at a higher billing rate?

- Would the risk and cost to the company be mitigated by the advantages of finishing on time so that other projects could move forward, or could a deliverable be delayed without much consequence?

When looking at these types of decisions over hundreds or thousands of different efforts, it becomes clear that companies need to take a structured, analytical approach to the matching of individuals, not just to one project, but to the portfolio of projects across the company.

Apply a Conceptual Model to Guide the Analysis

The shift toward a more analytic approach to balancing the number of employees with the work that needs to be accomplished requires a conceptual model that drives the planning process we described at the beginning of this chapter. The model includes:

- Projecting the demand for workers with needed capabilities.

- Determining the supply of workers to fill the roles.

- Identifying and resolving gaps between supply and demand to build an inventory of workers.

Projecting the Demand for Workers with Specific Capabilities

Translating the financial, sales, and growth objectives of a company into the demand for workers is the first step in the process.

Unfortunately, many organizations evaluate the demand for employees on an ad hoc basis or simply react to some immediate surpluses or shortages of talent. As the chief human resource officer of a large Canadian company reported, "Resource actions are our preferred planning tool!" A company can avoid this by using reasonable estimates and business plans that senior executives have already constructed for the purposes of establishing business objectives, budgets, and investor guidance.

The first step is to translate sales and cost projections into a reasonable estimate of the required number of workers, their capabilities, and their costs. In most cases, the typical staffing levels to deliver those products and services can be derived from historical data, that is, how much have we produced in the past, and what were the staffing requirements to produce it? The sales projections need not be precise; in fact, since they are based on probabilities, they cannot be precise. The randomness of events generally smooths out the prediction curve, as some orders may be canceled, others greatly modified, and still others come along unexpectedly.

Developing a model from historical data helps develop staffing profiles and performance standards for specific business units or projects. Once established, these templates can be used to derive staffing levels by running a series of scenarios that vary the amount and types of work that are projected over the next year or two and studying the resulting staffing levels required to accomplish the work. For example, as Cappelli observes in *Talent On Demand*, Station Casinos, a resort and casino developer and operator, has built a staffing model for casinos that allows it to project the demand for workers based on the number of casinos it is planning to open. The model identifies how many employees it needs to hire and train. The model also projects the number of advancement and leadership opportunities for

PROJECTING DEMAND

A medium-size life sciences company recognized it was constrained in its ability to conduct clinical trials.[a] The number of trials it needed to conduct was growing rapidly, as was the perceived need for employees and contractors to execute these trials. At the same time, there was also a lack of clarity in individuals' roles and responsibilities on projects, making it difficult to assign them to multiple efforts. Given the projected growth of the company, the associated costs of staffing these trials would soon become untenable.

To address this issue, the company began to estimate how many projects of each type would be in the pipeline over a three- to five-year period and then identified the demand for each role based on project type. This data allowed the firm to estimate demand for each role and, thus, skill set, and ultimately determine hiring needs. At the same time, the firm started classifying employees by skill type and developing roles based on the various skill categories. It then identified

---

current employees who are familiar with the company's operations.[6]

Determining the Supply of Workers to Fill the Roles

How does a company ensure that it will have the workforce it will need to succeed? It must perform supply projections for the same units and job categories reflected in the demand projections. Clearly, it is essential for HR to have a clear and consistent view of the capabilities, expertise, experience, and costs of the employees by role and tracked employee allocations by project. As a result, it could deploy resources when and where needed to more cost effectively staff projects.

This more structured, data-driven approach enabled the company to forecast equivalent full-time employee needs for permanent, contractor, and outsourced work. This activity- and role-based approach brought more rigor to short- and long-term workforce planning. It also equipped resource managers with the data to assign work to individuals with the appropriate skill sets. The company now deploys employees much more effectively by explicitly estimating and recognizing workforce peaks and troughs and assigning new project work that fits with availability and expertise. This effort has allowed the company to quantify its longer-term workforce needs, reducing costs through a better understanding of when to allocate work to employees, use short-term contractors, or outsource.

a. "Unlocking the DNA of the Adaptable Workforce," The IBM Global Human Capital Study, 2008.

current inventory of workers, while accepting that the inventory is dynamic. Some people will leave, but the workers who stay will also change. They will acquire new capabilities; they will transfer to other organizational units or be promoted to other jobs. Determining workforce supply must focus not only on turnover, but also on the flow of people through the organization and how promotions, transfers, and reorganizations will affect the supply of workers in various roles.

At the same time, companies must regularly monitor the external labor supply to identify the potential for bringing in workers from outside. Costs for acquisition of workers need to be compared among the options for hiring, contracting, outsourcing, or using temporary workers. Those costs need to be fully loaded to include not only salary and benefits for the workers, but the costs of acquisition, training, and severance (which can be quite high in some countries), so that they can be fairly compared. The cost and the availability of workers will clearly vary by local labor markets.

Qantas is an example of an organization that was forced to closely examine its supply of pilots. In the mid-2000s, the organization recognized that it was potentially facing a shortage of pilots, as the growth of low-cost regional airlines in the Asia-Pacific region was creating additional demand for pilots. To conduct the analysis, it examined a range of different variables that affected both the supply and demand for pilots.

On the demand side, Qantas looked at the projected growth rates of each of the four brands it operated (Qantas, QantasLink, Jetstar, Jetconnect) and the expected number of pilots required for different aircraft within the overall fleet. It then examined the attrition rates across different brands and aircraft, as well as the number of pilots who participated in training that allowed them to be rated across different aircraft. Qantas used this data to build a combined pilot resource model, which identified that there would be a need to recruit over eight hundred additional pilots, given the anticipated levels of growth. This information was critical to developing a human resource capacity plan, which we discuss in the next section.

Identifying and Resolving Gaps Between Supply and Demand to Build an Inventory of Workers

Once a company has projected the supply and demand for employees, it needs more analyses to explore alternatives for closing the inevitable gaps. These analyses may focus on using surplus workers to fill positions for which they are more or less qualified to fill, training workers to take new positions, bringing in temporary workers to fill short-term needs, or working with an outsourcing partner to cover peak loads. The company needs to compare these options against their costs, time to accomplish, and associated risks. Making these determinations requires optimization models that factor in not only the cost and timing of alternatives to fill the demand, but also the costs to the larger business of failing to fill the demand. By focusing on measuring the value of delivering the necessary inventory of workers, the organization can more effectively rationalize the human capital investments and operating costs it needs to deliver on its strategy. Analytics helps resolve these costs, benefits, and associated risks by asking the following questions:

- Can we fill positions from sources that are adequate, but less frequently used?

- How will filling positions with less qualified but perhaps less costly workers affect the productivity of the unit, the quality of production, and customer satisfaction?

- Can we mitigate the cost of layoffs by retraining workers? Can this be done within the needed time frame? Will those in the surplus pool want to do the new work and how will we train them?

- How can we be assured that contractors are capable of doing the work at the levels required?

- Will the use of contractors have a negative effect because they will leave with critical information about the company or deny development opportunities to permanent employees?

The output of this analytical optimization process is a resource-fulfillment plan that the company can use in the short term to guide managers in accessing the current inventory of workers and determine what actions HR should take to fulfill intermediate and long-term needs.

Capture Relevant Data

The analyses needed to build supply-and-demand projects clearly require data from many sources, including sales, marketing, operations, finance, as well as human resources. The results from the analyses then determine the inputs for resolving the gaps between supply and demand, and highlight the actions required to build and maintain the necessary inventory of workers and monitor their deployment.

Among the key sources of information needed to evaluate the demand for talent are:

- *Forecasted demand for products and services.* This forecast requires obtaining estimates of the products and services needed to meet the company's budget and financial goals and translate that work into staffing models. The relationship between the types and volumes of work is derived by merging data from very different sources. Depending on the nature of the business, the data for the volume of work is found in different transactional systems, such as point-of-sale systems, call-center applications, or, in the case of large project-based organizations, a list of engagements, project plans, or production runs for manufacturing firms. The number and types of workers and the hours required come from HR systems, payroll, and project time records. Linking these disparate systems is often very difficult because they lack common keys or reference points for integrating the information, or the data simply does not exist.

- *Other forecasted obligations for workers' time.* All too often, organizations fail to plan time in their projects for when their employees will be on vacation, sick, or in training. While these factors affect the supply of workers, they can be more easily described in the planning process as competing demands for workers' time. A company can derive this information from payroll data, time, and attendance, learning management systems, and systems that track training requirements and course time for licensing and certifications.

- *Task-related time and effort.* How long will an employee or team with specific skills and capabilities, on average, take to accomplish a particular task or project, such as completing a sale, restocking a department, fixing a water-main break, or producing a car? This information can be derived empirically from a number of industry-specific technologies that track activities and facilitate data collection. It can also be derived from the process, role design, and activity-based costing, described in chapter 2. Validation of these standards in service industries is often a manual process requiring some form of job analysis or time-and-motion studies to determine the appropriate work effort.

Similarly, calculating the supply of talent will require data regarding:

- *Worker skills, capabilities, and costs.* This taxonomy is critical to matching supply with demand as it connects the capability of the worker or team to the job requirements. In routine jobs, the skill sets can be precise and relatively easy to standardize and capture. For more knowledge-intensive positions, there will be less precision, but the ability for employees to adapt their skills to a variety of work demands will often be broader. Most HR and talent management systems have the capacity to store this information, but a surprising number of companies do not maintain standardized, measurable, capability assessments of their workers. Those that do have capability assessments link the maintenance and updating of this information to formal yearly evaluations and assessments and/or rely on workers to update their capabilities through online résumés or social media (e.g., LinkedIn).

- *Worker task and scheduling preferences.* Employees can provide input on their preferences for shift time, desired number of hours, assignment, mobility, career goals, vacation, and other factors that could influence their mobility, availability, and willingness to assume new roles in new locations.

- *Worker performance.* This information should measure an employee's or team's productivity, the quality of production, and costs. It allows organizations to make trade-offs in how to allocate individuals who have demonstrated potential strengths and/or opportunities for improvement. This data does not just refer to the annual assessments that are direct feedback from managers or peers available in HR or performance management systems. It refers to measures derived by merging information from sales or operational systems that determine the quality and volume of production.

Apply Analytical Methods

Some basic analytical tools are required to examine supply and demand and build and deploy the needed inventory of workers. All the tools have been available for many years; each has its strengths and weaknesses. The application of the tools does not precisely predict the future, but rather enables a company to anticipate what will likely happen and prepare for it.

Using Scenario Planning to Predict Workforce Demand

Almost all corporate planning and budgeting are based on a projection of sales by quarter. Often, these projections are based on a variety of assumptions about competitions, economic conditions, and consumer preferences. The predictions are based on models that start with a set of facts and relationships regarding what is known to have worked in the past. Using these models and projecting how factors in those models may change allows a company to assess the impact of the changes on its future. For example, AutoNation, a major automobile retailer, used scenario planning to avoid the recent crisis in car sales. Mike Jackson, AutoNation's chairman and chief executive officer, ran models that helped anticipate the events of 2008 and 2009. As a result, his company achieved profitability and positive cash flow during a period when many dealerships failed.[7]

A company can apply the same process to estimating the demand for labor. By linking the various scenarios that produced the sales projections and budget to the productivity standards of the workers and teams, it can accurately predict staffing levels by business unit, role, location, and cost. Running several scenarios of various product and service mixes can help a great deal in understanding the overall size, variety, and composition of the workforce. For instance, a systems integrator may wish to develop a variety of scenarios based on the size and types of projects to see what will have the greatest impact on the number, diversity, and timing of the skills required to deliver those projects. If the projects share many of the same capabilities, the task may be merely to obtain more of the same skills that already exist. If the projects require a diverse set of skills that are of limited supply within the organization, the effort may need to focus on building new areas of capability.

Applying Models to Determine the Labor Supply

Predicting the supply of labor requires understanding the flow of workers into, through, and out of the organization. Every year, as part of the normal course of business, managers throughout a company move people to new jobs and assignments and replace them with others. Many times, the movement of one worker sets up a chain of events that may provide new opportunities for several others. Most often, these positions are filled with obvious candidates, as coworkers acquire new skills, making them more capable, productive, and deserving of the vacant position. The effort of predicting the supply and demand of workers is not to anticipate every opening and every candidate who will fill the opening. That effort goes far beyond the mathematics of modeling and the administrative capability of HR departments. Predicting the supply and demand is directed at understanding the natural dynamics of the labor market and where and when that natural flow of workers through the company will fail to meet its needs. The flow is predictable, based on workers' length of service, performance, compensation, and past mobility. These factors influence the conditional probability of making transitions within or out of the organization.

The following example from a large global airline illustrates this approach. The airline analyzed how workers moved through twenty-five major job groups in more than eighty locations over a period of years that included a full range of market and economic conditions—periods of rapid growth and others of contraction. It calculated the rates based not only on economic conditions, but also the age and length of service of employees. This gave accurate estimates of the rates at which people could be expected to leave the company, transfer to different jobs and locations, or be promoted. Based on the market and economic conditions in the business plan, the company could use these estimates to project how many people it could expect to leave each of those major job groups by location, as well as how many it could expect to fill those positions and where they would come from. This projection produced a very simple summary by job and location.

A projection for the airline's sales force shows that the pools of qualified and interested workers who normally supplied the talent from within the company would be more than adequate to fill the demand for sales professionals in year one but would fall short in year two, by a substantial amount (see table 3-1). The system could disaggregate these pools to highlight the cause of the shortfall and suggest interventions to fix it by pointing out underutilized sources of supply to draw on.

TABLE 3-1

Projected sales force supply and demand

Year	Starting	Termina-tions	Transfers out	Those remaining	Transfers in	Natural result	Number needed
1	431	20	17	394	181	575	561
2	561	25	24	512	110	622	681

CONSTRUCTING A HUMAN RESOURCE CAPACITY PLAN AT QANTAS

Qantas had to develop a fulfillment plan to deal with a projected shortfall of qualified pilots. It developed a model of the current and future supply of pilots that looked at a wide range of factors. The model included an examination of:

- The total number of pilots, both in local markets and around the world, who were rated on the various aircraft Qantas flew.

- The global production of new aircraft and the number of pilots needed to operate them.

- The number of private training schools that developed commercial pilots.

- The number of military pilots in Australia and the percentage of those who chose to become civilian pilots once they left the military.

- The number of students in Qantas's own cadet program, which was a company-sponsored academy that attracted secondary school graduates wanting careers in aviation.

- The capability of its twelve-week intensive training program, which prepared individuals with commercial licenses to obtain certification to transport passengers.

From this supply analysis, Qantas found that there were many points that inhibited its ability to obtain the number of pilots it needed to address anticipated growth. For one, the airline industry was doing little to stimulate interest in careers in the aviation industry, therefore limiting how many individuals were considering aviation as a career. It also found that developing partnerships with a few feeder flight-training schools could potentially increase the number of pilots guided toward Qantas. It also found that its own recruitment processes, which involved coordination across five different brands, added to the unnecessary complexity of sourcing and hiring new pilots.

Based on the insights that it gathered from this long-term workforce planning exercise, Qantas determined that it had to more aggressively recruit pilots, particularly those with local backgrounds, from competitors outside the country. It also had to extend its relationships with training schools to capture a greater share of students graduating. Finally, it needed to streamline and focus its online recruitment efforts to ensure that potential pilots found it easy to express interest in the airline and minimize difficulty in applying.

Incorporating Optimization Techniques to Close Gaps

There are inevitable mismatches between the current internal labor force and the labor force that the company needs. In addressing these mismatches, a company needs to balance the costs, benefits, and risks associated with layoffs, hiring and training, and using contractors, temporary workers, and outsourcing partners. By attaching costs, benefits, and risks to the various options, the company can use methods of optimization or the mathematics of linear programming to find the best combination

TABLE 3-2

Optimizing choices to fill position

Source	Cost	Time to fill	Risk	Benefit
Hire perma-nent employess	What is the fully loaded cost of each solution?	What if the resources are not available?	Are they available?	Immediate quarterly effect on the bottom line.
Temporaries		Can we execute without these resources and for how long?	Will they engage?	Long-term effect on our brand
Contractors			Do they have	
Outsourcing			the skills?	
Retain key employees			At what cost?	
			Will they stay?	
Retain and develop sur-plus employees			Will they want to learn?	
Reorganize/automate work			Can we exe-cute in time?	

of actions to address surpluses and shortfalls. Once it makes this analysis, it can develop a human resource capacity plan to find the solution with the potential for the most benefit and the lowest cost and risk. These choices are summarized in table 3-2.

Present Statistical Findings to Stakeholders

Taking an analytic approach to addressing employee supply and demand goes beyond simply providing employees with a computerized schedule and/or project assignment list. It can set off a wide range of reactions by both managers and employees. The results of this ongoing analysis may have direct impact on employees' job duties, requirements, pay, and lives. In other situations, those closest to the work may view the reliance on analytical models as limiting their control and discretion. Therefore, key stakeholders need to be involved at all stages of an initiative that addresses talent supply-and-demand issues. In particular, three groups of key stakeholders require special attention:

- *Frontline employees.* While improvements to workforce planning can offer some benefits to employees (such as employee self-service and the ability to provide input into preferences), workers can perceive these modifications negatively. Many employees, hearing about the introduction of new workforce scheduling practices, will be concerned that the new processes will reduce their hours, limit their amount of overtime pay, or create nonstandard working shifts that affect their work-life balance. In fact, analytics can produce solutions to staffing problems that meet all the needs of the business, but are impossible for workers to perform.

  While many of these concerns are valid, companies can put strategies in place to mitigate them. For one, they can involve workers in developing work standards not only to learn what challenges they face in their jobs, but also to teach them the purpose of planning or scheduling systems. These sessions can help tailor the systems and address workers' concerns by improving the initial systems' requirements. They can also help managers understand how they can use the systems effectively to meet workforce concerns and the requirements of the business.

- *Managers.* As we saw in the initial case study of the oil foremen in chapter 1, first-line managers who have traditionally had responsibility for workforce scheduling may see these changes as threatening their jobs and reducing their control over scheduling decisions. They may believe that any form of centralized scheduling will not consider their knowledge of the local marketplace and, therefore, have limited benefits for their particular location. In a project-based environment, they may feel they are losing control of the resources they have significantly invested in training and mentoring. Managers may be concerned that, given the complexity of the system, they will be unable to use the technology effectively or articulate to employees the rationale behind scheduling and allocation decisions.

An analytical approach to managing the business will change the job of every manager. Consequently, companies have included local managers in the implementation and customization of the software so that the parameters of the system and the supporting processes focus on meeting the local needs that the managers and workers are addressing. Having managers prototype the processes and systems during the early implementation can reduce the possibility that they will simply abandon the new systems and processes.

One specialty retailer found value in providing a three-part education series to its store managers when it decided to upgrade its labor-scheduling system. The first part focused on building foundational skills, so that store managers understood the fundamental business model and the rationale for the new system. The second part educated managers on the new labor-scheduling policies and procedures, which helped clarify the business rules for development of new schedules. Finally, hands-on application experience allowed managers to refine the store-level optimization models. The retailer thought that by separating the discussions of the concepts and procedures from the use of the software itself, managers would be less inclined to form negative associations between the new policies and the actual technology implementation.

- *Unions and works councils.* Given the potential impact on the salaries of many employees, organizations with collective bargaining agreements need to pay special attention to the concerns of unions and works councils. Education, communication, and involvement of the union leaders early in the process are critical to addressing concerns. In addition, a company should consider identifying opportunities for workforce redeployment, increased cross-training, and gain-sharing opportunities to improve the likelihood for greater acceptance among relevant stakeholders.

Define Action Steps to Implement the Solution

In the previous steps, we focused on the need to determine the supply and demand for talent and an initial inventory of required employees. Relatively few individuals with the necessary tools and access to the data are needed to perform this task. However, to use the analyses to more tactically manage the workforce requires an infrastructure that enables operating personnel to make ongoing decisions.

To effectively manage and deploy the workforce on an ongoing basis, a company must be able to accomplish three tasks. First, it needs to monitor the human resource capacity plan as well as the inventory levels of workers and their utilization. Second, it must match workers to the openings and prioritize how to fill the openings. Finally, it must assess the utilization and efficacy of the deployment process. Done in concert, these three activities allow the company to constantly fine-tune the inventory to meet the demand for workers and balance the cost of maintaining the inventory with its effective utilization.

To make these fact-based decisions, a company needs processes and tools to determine the appropriate mix of skills required at any given time or place, including:

- *Standardized role and capability descriptions*, which help the organization more easily aggregate individuals with similar capabilities. In many companies, job descriptions evolve much like the tax code, with dozens of different variations appearing for very similar positions. Many companies, such as IBM, have seen value in rationalizing the number of job descriptions, making it easier to understand the true inventory of individuals in any given position. At one point, IBM had several thousand job categories, which over the years has been consolidated to several hundred. A joint team of HR and operations professionals now manages this effort on an ongoing basis; it introduces new positions through a review and approval process, while eliminating others that are less relevant.

- *Decision support tools that help managers make assignments dynamically from the inventory.* These tools help managers determine the costs of possible staffing alternatives by, for example, comparing the cost of filling a position with a contractor versus an employee. The tools also incorporate decision rules that balance the needs of the individual manager and employee with those of the company. This balance includes disciplined and data-driven allocation of scarce resources to their highest use within the company, while preventing costly bidding wars. This ensures continuity in business organizations and projects so that workers are not constantly being shifted before

MEASURES OF THE PROCESS FOR MANAGING A WORKFORCE INVENTORY

- Length of time to fill openings—indicating a lack of supply or a failure in the labor exchange.

- Utilization of the inventory by capability—indicating an oversupply of workers with no job openings.

- Cost of the workforce inventory.

- Quality of the inventory, including contractors and out-sourced workers.

- Analysis of managers' choices in terms of the cost and capabilities' match between position requirements and the worker chosen to fill the position, based on the available inventory. Are managers making the optimal decisions? If not, is it the result of how they are using the tools or are the tools not functioning as designed?

- Market integrity measures—are managers representing the work and conditions accurately? Are workers representing their capabilities and willingness to do the work accurately?

they can add value and enables allocation of workers to critical positions that are open because of undesirable job characteristics. The tools also incorporate scheduling constraints in the form of collective bargaining work rules, government regulations, and workers' capabilities and willingness to adjust to extended or odd work hours.

ALLOCATING WORKERS: IBM AND ITS WORKFORCE MANAGEMENT INITIATIVE

In 2003, IBM set out to transform its workforce management processes, starting with its global population of consulting services professionals. As we noted in the beginning of the chapter, a key component of this transformation was the development of its workforce management initiative (WMI) which provided a framework for aligning the systems, policies, capacity management, and deployment processes as well as the technical architecture needed to increase talent effectiveness on a global scale. Early in the effort, IBM leveraged its experience in supply chain management and recognized similarities in how it configured orders for complex systems and how it could adapt these ideas in putting together client project teams.

Similar to the example of the community college that we highlighted in chapter 2, a core component of the WMI was the development of an expertise taxonomy or capability framework that classifies the skills of practitioners in a standardized fashion. This collection of expertise data provides valuable input into two other important components of the WMI: "Professional Marketplace" and the "Resource Capacity Planning Optimizer" (RCP).

Professional Marketplace is an internal application in which managers can request individuals for projects, as well as view a potential pool of candidates who are available for assignments. This tool also gives internal job seekers a list of potential projects that are currently being staffed and allows them to apply for the positions. Prior to the introduction of Professional Marketplace, staffing managers, who worked from individual spreadsheets and had little or no visibility into resources beyond their particular region or practice, identified and selected workers. They did not have the tools to model the cost implications of various trade-offs and economic decisions. Professional Marketplace enables project managers, project seekers, and intermediaries to see the market for talent and reduce the administrative requirements for matching individuals to projects.

How does Professional Marketplace work?[a] Typically, it starts with a project manager's request for a specific job role and skill set, the expected duration of the assignment, the cost-recovery rate of the individual, and any specific location and language requirements, as well as unstructured information about the particular job. The system compares this information against a repository of skills, résumés, interests, availability, and cost information. It generates a list of potential candidates who match or closely match the structured attributes. The system will also recommend individuals who may not exactly meet the project specification (e.g., someone who has worked in the railroad versus the airline industry) or who may be located closer to the project site.

If no candidates are found with the needed skill sets, the project manager can create an "open seat" describing the needs of the position, which becomes accessible to staffing and resource managers and other employees across the company. Once the position becomes visible, either employees can nominate themselves to fill the position or staffing intermediaries can recommend people within their groups.

While Professional Marketplace is designed to more effectively match the immediate need for staffing professionals to jobs, the RCP helps workforce planners determine which types of resources are anticipated, given a projected level of customer demand.[b] By looking at a history of similar assignments, the RCP generates a standard "bill of materials" for a specific type of project and then determines whether there are sufficient resources within the firm to deliver on these types of engagements over time. Not only can the program determine if there are gaps or gluts in one particular skill set, but it can also develop scenarios to see how they can be rectified by providing training opportunities to employees with similar skill sets. The RCP provides workforce planners with insight into whether they need to hire outside resources (either as full-time employees or contractors) or whether they can build internal resources to match the expected demand.

a. Daniel Connors and Aleksandra Mojsilovic, "Workforce Analytics for Services Economy," in *Handbook of Service Science*, edited by James Sphorer, Paul Maglio, and Cheryl Kieliszewski (New York: Springer, 2010).

b. D. L. Gresch, D. P. Connors, J. P. Fasano, and R. J. Wittrock, "Applying Supply Chain Optimizing Techniques to Workforce Planning Problems," *IBM Journal of Research and Development* 51, no. 3 (2007): 251–261.

- *Evaluation tools and metrics to measure both the success of matching workers to business needs and process improvement.* These metrics include measures to determine how well the allocation process is performing (see the sidebar) and measures of success such as overall productivity; sales per cost of labor hour of the business unit, team, or shift; and overall customer satisfaction and quality of the product.

Cross-functional involvement is critical to building an effective human capital supply chain. In most organizations, the operations function has primary responsibility for the day-to-day balancing of resources to maintain production or service clients. However, other support areas are critical to this process as well. As we saw in chapter 2, HR professionals can play an important role in the development of a common expertise taxonomy, which is needed to identify transferable skills and capabilities. Also, HR can help to address the overall people issues associated with the migration toward a more flexible workforce. For example, if a company decides to increase the number of part-time shifts as a result of an improved labor-scheduling and deployment capability, it will also have to consider the need to dip into different labor pools to find individuals interested in part-time work, adjust compensation and benefits to attract part-time workers, revise the training content and training hours to get new workers up to speed, and guide supervisors who will have to manage more employees. In all these areas, HR can have an important supporting role.

In addition to HR, other departments contribute to an organization's ability to manage an effective inventory of workers. The legal function ensures that regulatory statutes and employee agreements are incorporated into the decision rules used by optimization programs. IT manages and hosts the applications needed to run internal labor exchanges and other relevant software products as well as integrates various systems that feed workforce planning applications. The finance organization ensures that the cost data used to make assumptions about labor standards and budgets is accurate and reflects the actual business environment.

Efficient Allocation of Workers to Where They Are Most Needed

We have seen a trend toward internal labor markets as a way of managing workforce inventory and deployment with respect to project- or schedule-driven work. Airline, retail, construction, hospital, insurance, banking, and computer service industries as well as industries with many professionals in R&D, such as pharmaceuticals, electronics, aerospace, and defense, use internal exchanges. These clearinghouses bring together projects looking for resources, and employees wanting to work on projects. Internal exchanges match individuals with project opportunities and provide critical data to evaluate eventual imbalances in supply and demand for talent. They are an effective and efficient substitute for centralized command and control of the company's resources.

In addition to being efficient ways of allocating talent, labor exchanges give workers incentives to develop their capabilities, while meeting the current and future needs of the business. Companies with systematically structured work and capability frameworks can give workers access to information that describes the progression of roles through job families and lays out the capabilities and performance levels required. This makes career paths more visible and keeps workers informed about the connection between their jobs and the main goals of the company.

Conclusion

In today's global business environment, organizations are more likely than ever to be moving into new markets and geographies to tap into new sources of talent and take advantage of labor arbitrage. At the same time, they are moving toward more knowledge-intensive, project-based work that requires the creation and dismantling of work units on an ongoing basis. Increasing customer demands are also bringing greater attention to the scheduling and deployment of frontline workers. All these forces represent a shift in the way that organizations think about allocating and deploying their workforce. Those companies able to make better decisions about where and when they need their workers will be more likely to improve productivity over the long haul.

Balancing talent supply and demand is an ongoing juggling act, involving multiple functions, tools, stakeholders, and outcomes. But what is consistent across all of these areas is the need for a quantitative approach to understanding the various drivers, the costs associated with managing inventory and fulfilling (or not fulfilling) customer needs, and the opportunities associated with more effective allocation of resources. Also central is a common approach to classifying skills and capabilities. Without this, it is nearly impossible to categorize and analyze the inflows and outflows of talent. In addition, organizations must develop the skills and capabilities to interpret the ongoing stream of data and make strategic choices about the sourcing, development, and retention of talent from around the globe.

CHAPTER FOUR

Untangling the Drivers of Workforce Performance

"I love this company, but it is frustrating. I just want to succeed. I want the opportunity to show what I can do. I just need to know *what* to do: be given the tools to succeed and be told whether I am doing OK and how to improve."

—A customer service representative talking about the difficulties of her work

In 2008, Sprint seemingly hit rock bottom, reporting a $29.7 billion write-down on goodwill, cutting four thousand jobs, and seeing a 50 percent reduction in its stock price. Once a champion of customer service, Sprint had seen a steady decline in its customer satisfaction ratings; by 2008, Sprint was ranked well below its competitors. Sprint customers called for assistance twice as often as customers of its competitors. First-call resolution was poor. When customers called, the average time to speak to an agent was nearly seven minutes, fourteen times the industry average. Over one-third of the callers simply hung up. To solve these urgent performance problems, Sprint used an analytical framework similar to the one we are advocating.

Sprint executives decided they had to reestablish the reputation for superior service that had been the company's major selling point. Using available data and a structured, but simple set of analytical techniques, Sprint accurately identified the drivers of performance and customer satisfaction. It recognized the immediate steps it could take to improve customer satisfaction and retention, as well as what actions it needed to take in the long run to ensure that customer service provided ongoing competitive advantage.

In the short run, the results of its analysis showed the highest-performing agents' key behaviors, how they were most successful in dealing with their customers, and how supervisors could immediately leverage these behaviors to help agents who were having difficulty achieving the same results. In the long run, the analysis showed Sprint how to align the efforts of the entire company to achieve a culture oriented toward customer service. The effort went beyond the immediate boundaries of the call centers Sprint directly controlled and included collaboration with its outsourced service providers. It eventually included taking a more horizontal approach, incorporating customer support as part of the design of the product and service offerings.

How does a company get its employees to enthusiastically work at the required levels of quality and quantity? The previous two chapters are the basis for asking this question. Chapter 2 described how companies use analytics to define what they need from workers, as well as what they must offer them in terms of structuring work intelligently, making performance standards clear and measurable, and creating rewards that would reinforce appropriate behavior. This defines not only what activities and objectives a company expects of the worker, but also how it will support that work by a rational division of labor and enabling technology. If the work is designed well, the company will not only profit but also give workers a sense of accomplishment and opportunity.

Chapter 3 focused on how companies can find workers who are interested and able to perform at the required level within a specific corporate environment by recruiting, hiring, developing, and deploying the right number of workers at the right time and cost. If these activities are successful, the company will find not only capable workers, but also people who fit the company culture and respond well to the intrinsic and extrinsic rewards of the position.

Unfortunately, even after putting in significant effort to ensure the work is defined well and the workers they recruit are capable, many companies find that their workforces are not delivering the competitive performance required to succeed. Too often, companies inadvertently lose sight of what they need to do to achieve their competitive goals because of incremental changes to:

- Technology, and the adoption of new tools and processes

- Markets, and the introduction of new products and services

- Organizational changes

- Financially driven decisions, such as outsourcing and the shifting of work to other geographies

As a consequence, what was intended to improve performance at one period in time may, in some cases, have the opposite effect.

In some situations, the underlying cause of poor performance is not readily apparent and cannot be linked to a specific event. It may involve the breakdown of the implicit contract between the company and workers that goes far beyond the exchange of work for wages. A maturing workforce may lead to a fundamental change in the needs or capabilities of the workers. Over time, supervisors may lose sight of the intended spirit and purpose of performance metrics and find ways to achieve the metrics that subvert their original intentions. In these situations, companies need a more comprehensive analytic approach that considers the complexity of relationships associated with how they manage and deploy workers; changes in the capabilities and needs of the workforce and the supporting organization structure; the nature and demands of the work; problems in the selection, training, and development of the workforce; and performance metrics and their use.

Two Drivers of Performance

We use two case studies to illustrate two important drivers of performance: one case looks at the connection between performance measures and actual performance, the other examines the underlying factors that drive motivation and higher productivity. Both case studies deal with call centers that are critical to each company's competitive success. Each case follows our six-step framework for organization and workforce analytics established in the first three chapters.

Understanding the Drivers of Performance at Sprint

The simple and straightforward use of analytics helped Sprint make great strides in improving its customer service by focusing on the performance of its call centers and agents. This case highlights how Sprint dealt with its internal workforce as well as outsourced partners, a fact of life in a global economy.

Frame the central problem

As we discussed earlier, Sprint was facing a crisis in serving its customers. It recognized that it had structural problems—the complexity of its market offerings and the technology it used to support its customer service agents—that would take a long time and a large investment to solve. Unfortunately, time and money were not available; it had to act immediately to stop the loss of customers and get to the point where its reputation was not a barrier to adding customers. By examining the underlying metrics that were driving agent behavior, the incentives in the contracts of its providers of outsourced services, and the qualities that differentiated high performers across the organization, Sprint was able to quickly identify both increased efficiencies and achieve higher levels of customer satisfaction.

Apply a conceptual model to guide the analysis

Sprint's approach to improving customer service was simple and direct. First, it believed that agents felt they were subject to a "whack-a-mole metric of the month" management process. Direction was driven from the top and shifted from month to month. One month, managers believed the time that agents took to handle calls was too high and would develop metrics to focus on that. The next month, statistics on first-call resolution seemed low, so that would become the "new" performance metric. Next, the focus would be on credit adjustments or total satisfaction, and so on. The lack of consistency made it difficult for agents to become good at their work, given that the definition of what *good* meant changed constantly.

Second, after reviewing its internal policies, Sprint thought that its performance measures and compensation were not tied to delivering excellent customer service. Some performance measures were out of the agent's direct control. Consequently, focusing on what could be controlled, measuring it, and holding agents accountable became a key focus for the analysis. A similar lack of alignment among performance measures, rewards, and customer satisfaction was discovered in the service centers that had been outsourced. Vendors' rewards increased as the volume of customer calls went up, so, as a result, there was no incentive for first-call resolution or for reducing calls and increasing customer satisfaction.

Third, Sprint thought that it needed to build a more positive culture that invited the agents and first-line supervisors to act on what they could control. It believed that agents tended to blame outside "stuff" and feel victimized by what they could not control. This included the quality of their case and content management software, along with the variability of the different sales initiatives.

These systems and policies would take time to fix. Sprint had to identify the capabilities and behaviors of agents who were successful using the existing tool sets and addressing the current products and services in order to develop these capabilities in other agents. Eventually, it realized that marketing and sales efforts, in effect, defined the work that agents performed. The introduction of new products and services led to new metrics and the need to rapidly learn new sets of terms and conditions, billing, and service requirements. Sprint suspected that the constantly changing products and services it offered might be too variable and inconsistent, making it difficult for the agents and supervisors to keep up with the offerings and provide for consistently excellent customer service and performance.

In summary, Sprint focused its data gathering to understand and test how to improve customer satisfaction and retention by:

- Identifying what results the agents and vendors could control and what action they needed to take to improve customer service.

- Understanding what caused variation in agent performance.

- Creating a focused and clear set of consistent priorities and performance metrics.

- Aligning performance measures and rewards for the outsourced call centers and their own agents.

- Eventually reestablishing a customer service–oriented environment that extended across the company.

Capture relevant data

As Lonnie Johnston, director of performance management and analytics, said, "Sprint was awash in data." It needed "less, but more focused information that they could rely on" to make decisions rapidly and accurately. It had little technology that allowed for a structured approach to performance management. There were no consistent measures for call centers and sales offices. Operating in this void, managers focused on their instincts and the metrics they thought were important. This led managers to enforce conflicting policies and stress different procedures. There were no automated tools to guide their decisions; the acquisition of data was arduous, and its accuracy was always in question. Everything was manual, which meant that managers were expected to enter data and chase after information, taking time away from coaching and developing their teams and other key management activities. Remarkably, Sprint was able to acquire and track, by spreadsheets, more than eighty metrics that were inconsistent and often competing for attention. Integrating across these metrics required great effort.

Initially, Sprint decided to rethink what it was doing and start by simply gathering reliable data from one trusted source. It looked at "switch data," extracts from its call-center systems, which supplied detailed information about wait times, abandoned calls, the length of time agents spoke to customers, the amount of time customers were on hold, transferred calls, and the time the agent spent dealing with actions that resulted from the conversation with the customer. This data could be integrated with customer feedback from survey processes. Analysis of the combined data ultimately revealed what agents were doing within the system and what was driving customer satisfaction.

Ensuring the quality of the data required work. The accuracy and meaning of the data were often called into question, allowing managers and agents to explain away poor performance with anecdotal information. Poor, untimely, and inconsistent data led to passive resistance in accepting the results of the analysis. All arguments about the meaning and accuracy of the data were peeled away when the stakeholders were provided with what Johnston referred to as "a single source of the truth."

In addition to the data that was already being collected in the normal course of business, Sprint conducted additional studies to understand what contributed to the difference between high and low performers. It combined the performance of both high- and low-performing agents with data gathered through observing their behavior on the job. The behaviors included measures of typing ability, patterns of systems use, and client interaction. This data—captured, categorized, and then analyzed in a structured format—proved crucial in helping managers identify the areas that their agents needed to improve and how managers could coach them to higher performance.

Apply analytical methods

The analysis that Sprint performed was elegantly simple, targeted at identifying the relationships that drove performance. As Johnston reported, there was so much low-hanging fruit and the relationships were so obvious that advanced analytical techniques would not have increased the yield captured from the analysis. Examination of basic frequency distributions and simple cross-tabulations and correlations confirmed many of the hypotheses. The span between high and low performers was so obvious that no one could argue with the opportunity it presented.

The next step was to institute accountability measures that could track the ability of the manager and supervisors to affect the performance variation. Reducing this variation was central to driving overall improvement. Some evidence indicated that there was a correlation between the introduction of new complex products and services and increased call volumes, abandoned calls, and low first-call resolution. But the impact of the complexity of market offerings had to be weighed against the fact that many agents were quite capable of performing in the midst of this complexity. The analysis also showed that there were sharp differences with respect to the performance of the various call centers, indicating that it was worth harvesting the best practices and understanding the environment and management practices that led to higher performance and disseminating that information to other call centers. Another surprising finding occurred from interviews with agents. When asked what their goal was, agents reported that their job was to follow Sprint's processes and procedures, not to serve and satisfy customers.

Finally, the analysis of what behaviors differentiated good agents from poor agents indicated that agents could be divided into four groups. The top performers needed little or no help. The next group required limited intervention and coaching on behaviors that they could easily improve. The next group could, with effort, be brought up to speed but would require more assistance and time. The analysis showed that the lowest-performing group required too much time and effort and would detract from the supervisor's ability to improve the performance of the rest of his or her team.

Present statistical findings to stakeholders

Discussion of the findings from the analysis centered around three basic questions, given here in order of their immediacy. First, how could supervisors and managers of call centers effectively improve the performance of their agents and teams? The analysis of the agents' performance indicated that there were certain key behaviors that were typical of high-performing agents. These included typing speed, how they listened to and remembered key facts from their conversation with customers, and how they used the case management systems and searched the content databases that supported their conversations with customers. The results of this analysis were translated into coaching tools that supervisors used to more effectively develop their agents. The performance categories and their associated behaviors provided supervisors concrete steps and targeted information on whom and how to focus their efforts. This proved a valuable competitive tool. In addition, the application of the tools across all of the outsourced service centers would build a higher and more uniform level of service for Sprint's customers.

Second, how could performance metrics for agents be simplified, more focused, and improved? Sprint took efforts to improve the metrics relevance, timeliness, and accuracy and ensure that the agents could control the metrics by changing their behavior. Eventually, Sprint created a performance management system that allowed each center to see how it performed on a daily basis and drilled down to specific teams and agents. This system provided a single and trusted source of data regarding the performance of the agents, their teams, the centers, and the company. The system also allowed the agent to record and acknowledge individual assessments and coaching points. This formed a contract for improvement that tracked measurable and achievable steps toward the goal of improved performance.

Third, how could call volume be decreased by providing processes and incentives for everyone across the corporation to improve metrics, such as first-call resolution and customer satisfaction? This meant working horizontally across the service spectrum from the inception of a marketing idea through to its development, testing, and implementation and, finally, its support in the service centers. Formal reviews were instituted to ensure that new, more competitive product and service offerings could be supported after they were introduced, and by more explicitly anticipating the demands on the call-center tools, agents, and staffing.

Define action steps to implement the solution

Sprint took steps to roll out a simplified set of metrics across the company and its outsource providers. It reduced the number of metrics from eighty to twenty and developed tools to improve the skills of supervisors in translating the analysis and metrics into improved performance for all the call centers. Medium and low performers were provided targeted coaching on how to improve; if lower performers did not improve, they were dismissed from the company, using accurate performance data for evidence. The same rules applied to outsourced call centers. Low-performing call centers were coached on how to improve, their efforts were tracked, and if they did not improve, they were dropped. Sprint put in place automated tools to gather and clean data and provide the scorecards and metrics daily and accurately. This information supported more sophisticated, timely, and in-depth analysis, while professionals knowledgeable about Sprint's business, its data, and the appropriate techniques supported ana-lytical activities.

The improvement in performance and measurable business benefit was significant and impressive. Debates about the qual-ity and meaning of data were replaced by fact-based conversa-tions about how best to achieve increased performance. Management time and effort shifted from gathering data or arguing about reports to supervising and coaching agents. This reduced the resistance to change and efforts to improve per-formance. In addition, accurate data and the ability to analyze it and distribute the valuable metrics have helped Sprint attain its goals:

- Customer satisfaction is up 43 percent.

- First-call resolution is up 42 percent.

- Calls per subscriber are down 39 percent.

- Operations costs are down 34 percent.

- Billing adjustments are down 73 percent.

In short, increased performance and the productivity of agents have reduced the resources required and led to fewer, but more-effective call centers. Eleven call centers were eliminated in 2008, and twenty in 2009. As one call-center vice president stated, "An-alytics at Sprint was a catalyst for achieving substantial change and improvement in performance. The information provided formed a foundation for execution and basis for good leadership. The results of the analysis provided structure, organization, and rigor to our actions within each call center."

Understanding the Drivers of Employee Engagement at CORP

Much literature discusses the linkage between motivated, engaged employees and increasing financial benefit to the organization.[1] These studies address a myriad of factors, including the various drivers that motivate employees and the different measures of performance that they affect within the organization. There are also numerous companies, ranging from Sears to Sysco, that have documented the financial return associated with improving employee engagement.[2]

We do not seek to replicate these studies' results. Rather, we focus on identifying the analytical methods that companies can use to better understand issues involving employee engagement and motivation, and how they can apply the methods to solve real-world issues. Such an analytical approach is key to understanding how companies' strategies translate to the behaviors of their workforce. A critical piece of this analysis is an understanding of the broad interactions between workers and managers as they carry out daily operations. This interaction occurs in the context of the goals of the company, the structure of the work, the tools workers are given, and the implicit social contract that the company and the workers enter into.

Many companies find great benefit in continually evaluating whether they have an engaged and productive workforce. Periodic lack of alignment is inevitable; ignoring it will result in negative impact on the bottom line. The CORP case describes a framework for evaluating whether the implicit social contract is working well, determining where there are failures, and identifying solutions. It deals with a somewhat more complex and mysterious problem in which the cause was less clear and required some analytical detective work. The case illustrates the use of survey research, focus groups, and causal analysis in uncovering the problem. It ultimately points out the critical importance of the role of the first-line supervisor.

Often the causes of performance failures are not straightforward. Getting to the heart of the problem requires picking apart the causal connections and taking action. Many companies have invested significant amounts of money and effort developing performance measures and management strategies, only to find that their execution does not result in the expected outcomes. Their preliminary efforts to understand what is going on and what corrective action to take are often frustrating. These challenges became critical to CORP, which was losing customers and market share in an expanding market.[3] CORP's customer service representatives (CSRs) had critical roles in achieving customer satisfaction, customer retention, and increased revenue through direct sales of products and services. CORP found that its service centers were performing poorly and had unacceptably high rates of turnover.

The poor performance and high attrition were especially troubling since the company had spent considerable time and money in designing the CSR role and establishing the capabilities and behaviors required for success. It used the identified competencies to guide employee selection and training. It also tried to retain workers by offering very competitive pay and benefits.

The company had also worked hard to establish job-related, objective, observable, and balanced performance criteria to help develop its CSRs and serve as the basis for its financial incentives. In the spirit of "what gets measured gets done," metrics on customer satisfaction, sales, and processing time were fed back to CSRs and supervisors every month. Supervisors were expected to use this information to monitor and develop their employees; in fact, part of the supervisors' performance evaluation related to how many of their employees met or exceeded these published performance standards. To further support this process, a special improvement program was set up to assist CSRs who were having difficulty meeting their performance criteria.

Frame the central problem

The initial analysis of readily available data from CORP's HR and operational systems confirmed that the turnover rate for voluntary and involuntary reasons was very high, and that most of that turnover was occurring in the first six months of employment. Attrition rates showed strong negative correlation with performance; the poorer the performance, the more likely the CSR was to leave the company. Each month, 5 to 6 percent of employees receiving the lowest performance rating left, while 1 to 2 percent of the highest performers left (see figure 4-1). This association pointed to a high-performance-driven environment, where failing to achieve targets was not tolerated.

Over time, one would expect this extreme difference in turnover rates to lead to a very high-performing group of CSRs, especially those with more than one year of service. The cumulative rates of termination should eliminate 50 percent of those in the poorest category and only about 10 percent of those in the highest level. Yet, this did not happen. Unfortunately, the performance of those in their twelfth month of employment was no different from newly hired employees, despite programs designed to reward people who had done well, develop people

FIGURE 4-1

Tenure by performance levels

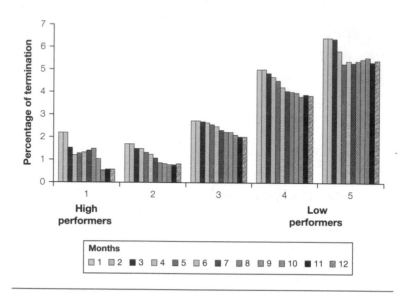

needing help, and eliminate those performing poorly. Not surprisingly, given this situation, there was no correlation between the monthly sales generated by a CSR and his or her length of service. This state of affairs was not only contradictory, but very frustrating, given the need for capable and effective workers to execute the company's business strategy. Additional facts added to the mystery. A regression analysis of available data from the human resource systems could not identify any variables that were predictive of the sales performance of *individuals* within the company. In contrast, it was possible to produce a model that predicted CSR *team* sales performance. The model contained five variables that had statistically significant relationships to sales:[4]

- Average length of service of the team

- Length of service of the supervisor of the team

- Compensation of the supervisor

- Performance rating of the supervisor

- Turnover rate of the team

The first variable, the average tenure of the team, had a powerful association with higher sales. This factor had three times the impact of the other four variables combined. For every month of increase in the average length of service of the team, the team was capable of selling $100,000 more in products and services. Across the company, this translated into the potential for adding more than $40 million of sales a year to the company. This effect was not apparent in the relationships manifested in individual data. What was happening at the team level that was not occurring at the individual level?

Two additional variables in the equation added to the puzzle. There was a negative relationship between the performance rating of the supervisor and the sales of the team. As the performance rating of the supervisor decreased, the sales of the team increased. Finally, and perhaps most puzzling, was the finding that as the *turnover of the team* increased, team sales increased. How could both increase in tenure and high turnover be significantly and positively associated with increased sales? CORP undertook further research to understand what was driving these results.

Apply a conceptual model to guide the analysis

It was critical for the company to understand the causes of high turnover if it was to retain high-performing CSRs and increase the average tenure of the teams and their productivity. It needed a combination of methods to solve the mystery. A well-designed survey was essential to illuminate the experience of newly hired CSRs and determine what factors could influence their retention, commitment, and performance. A set of focus groups targeted at specific populations and issues then discussed the results of the survey analysis. The groups developed a robust understanding of these issues, based on the experiences of the populations most affected.

Our experience has shown that there are eight fundamental dimensions that determine workforce engagement and thereby influence company performance. Each interacts with the others to determine the social contract under which the workers perform their jobs:

1. **Work design** must be efficient and reflect the quality and volume of work required for the company to meet its objectives.

2. **Performance measures** must be objective, observable, and directly connected to behaviors that the workers can control; the rewards for doing a good job must be sufficient to *reinforce* good performance.

3. **The talent sourcing and selection process** must succeed at hiring employees who are capable and motivated to do the work.

4. **The training and development activities** must support the knowledge and skills required to do the work and provide ways of acquiring those additional skills needed in the future.

5. **Workforce planning and allocation** must balance the demand for workers with supply and allocate resources where they are needed.

6. **Workers' individual needs** must be met.

7. **Leadership** must motivate workers.

8. **The culture of the workplace community** must demonstrate and encourage behavior that is positive, supportive, consistent, and fair.

Finally, if all of these dimensions are coordinated and executed well, the workers will be committed to the company and actively:

9. **Engaged** in achieving the mutually recognized goals.

Clearly, there is interdependence across all of these factors. The responsibilities and performance standards that define the work determine who to hire and how much they will cost. The brighter and more capable the employee, the more efficient training and development can be. The more capable and motivated the workforce, the less directive managers need to be and the more empowering the culture. Hiring less qualified workers than the job requires results in increased demands on training and supervision.

Capture relevant data

Surveys must be designed with great care to ensure sufficient clarity of issues to produce meaningful analysis.[5] It is important to build a survey that focuses on events and behaviors that are specific to the routine experiences of the workers and the timing of particular events in the company. Eliciting factual information about events that occurred, as well as employee reaction to those events, is essential. Also, the concepts that are the focus of analysis should not depend on only one or two questions. For instance, the scale that measured employee engagement for this survey was made up of the responses to six questions, five focused on employee behavior and one on employee attitudes.[6] This ensured that each concept had multiple measures, increasing the reliability and validity of the overall metrics. The subscales of the nine components of the factors on the engagement survey are described in some detail in appendix A.

The concepts and their detailed components represent a generalized approach to examining how engaged workers are with the company's objectives and what factors cause or inhibit that engagement. Every company will need to tailor and focus the questions in such a survey on its particular needs and situations. Building models that show how these factors directly affect engagement and how they interact with each other can show not only where the dysfunction is but what levers can be modified to improve performance. CORP was interested in understanding how the first eight factors listed earlier predicted or contributed to employee engagement. Scores on engagement scales were highly predictive of turnover, which was a primary interest of CORP.

The survey questions that measured these nine components were behavioral in nature and focused first on events and actions, and secondarily on attitudes or feelings. While some questions about attitudes and feelings are illuminating, the route that must be forged to accomplish change is through changing particular behaviors. For instance, in collecting information about employees' sense of being valued, CORP asked about actions that their supervisors and coworkers may have taken that would generally reflect being valued, and asked directly about their feelings. The questions were structured to get candid and serious responses by using language that reflected the daily vernacular of the workplace for this particular company and the concrete actions and events employees experienced on a daily basis.

Apply analytical methods

CORP selected a representative sample of employees with less than twelve months of service to complete the survey. Again, the focus of CORP's analysis was predicting the scores of respondents on the engagement scale, which in turn was highly predictive of employee turnover and performance. The responses to the important behavioral components of that scale were telling: close to 50 percent said they were planning to find another job, while over 30 percent reported that they were actively looking for a job or had already applied to another company.

From the data it collected, CORP was able to analyze what factors contributed to the engagement scale. This analysis gave it an estimate of how important each factor was in predicting the engagement scale. As can be seen in figure 4-2, by far the largest direct contributor to identifying the drivers of employee engagement was the ability of the organization to meet the CSRs' individual needs. This scale, which measured the extent to which CSRs felt they were valued, fairly compensated, and

FIGURE 4-2

Explaining the variance in engagement

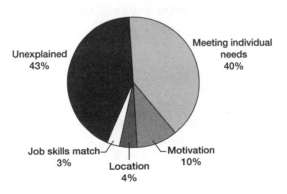

125

secure in their jobs, explained 40 percent of the variance in their engagement scores.

A scale that explained another 10 percent of the variance in engagement involved questions about employee motivation. This measured the extent to which the CSRs were willing to improve their performance, whether they would put in extra effort when needed, whether they were interested in advancing their careers, and whether their work was stimulating. There were other factors that contributed a small amount to the understanding of engagement. But, by far, the magnitude of the importance of meeting CSRs' needs focused on further exploring this issue.

Digging deeper into the analysis, CORP found that three critical sets of factors influenced whether CSRs felt that their individual needs were being met (see figure 4-3):

- The CSRs' view of the performance management system explained 41 percent of the total variance in meeting individual needs.

FIGURE 4-3

Company levers for meeting workers' needs

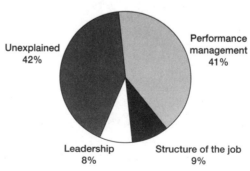

- The structure of the job and the tools they were given to do the job explained 9 percent of the total variance regarding individual needs being met.

- Leadership and supervisor support explained 8 percent of the total variance regarding individual needs being met.

Presenting statistical findings to stakeholders

By far, the largest direct contributor to meeting the CSRs' needs was how supervisors used the *performance management system*. This factor was measured by several sets of questions about the performance management process and the company's performance improvement plan. While most CSRs had no complaints about the performance standards per se, many expressed dissatisfaction with the lack of accuracy and reliability of the measurements themselves. Furthermore, many felt the consequences of missing their performance goals were not fair, nor were they consistently applied. Consider this quote from one CSR who participated in the focus groups:

Reps are concerned about the fairness of how they are scored on customer satisfaction. It is perceived as unfair. The score is based on only five customers a month. But the customer may be rating something other than the rep's customer orientation on the call. The customer may be thinking of the rep the call was transferred to.

The rapidly changing product line and the associated performance measures also caused the CSRs to challenge the fairness of the performance management process and their ability to adapt to it. This can be seen in the following CSR quote:

We would like to see less change. They ask you to push a product or service hard one day and then ask you to stop selling it the next. There is no advance warning about the changes. They simply occur.

CSRs also saw the improvement program as punitive, rather than an opportunity to receive help, as it was intended. One CSR commented:

It is very easy to get terminated here. Once you get on [the program], you are walking on thin ice. This is stressful. It is very short term. It does not matter how you did in the past. It is not about a relationship. You can be doing well for some time and then not hit your number one month.

Not only did the content of product lines and services constantly change, but the *reference tools* that were provided were not adequate to help CSRs keep up with the changes. The tools were incapable of delivering the necessary information needed to perform their jobs; they were painfully slow, navigation was poorly structured, and they provided inadequate information. CORP found that some managers were aware of the difficulty the CSRs were having:

Specialists need to know a lot to get through a call. It is difficult for them to get the answers they need from the systems. And they are under the spotlight to get it. If they do not get it right, they get hammered. This is a lot of pressure.

The demanding pace of the work and the poor tools they were given directly affected CSRs' ability to perform well and their self-esteem suffered. As one CSR described:

It is a challenge to get the information you need to answer the customer's questions . . . The knowledge management system does not help. It gives you tons of questions you need to wade through to get your answer. The answer should be at your fingertips. So you put the customer on hold. The systems make you feel incompetent.

The *tightly structured nature of the work* also played a significant role in restricting CSRs who were well trained and effective to scripted, narrow, and rigid interactions. One college-educated CSR commented:

They require you to follow strict scripts. You need to constantly recap. This makes you look dumb. You can feel this with the customer. You know when it is going well and you are connecting. But when you are required to repeat things, the customer thinks—why is he repeating this? You lose credibility. It makes the customer question your intelligence.

Finally, a critical element in meeting employee needs is *supervisor support*. The focus groups described the impact an immediate supervisor can have in how he or she either helps employees deal with problems or chooses to avoid them. Further, the focus groups highlighted the importance of basing the relationship between supervisor and employee on more than just the mechanical aspects of whether the CSR made his numbers. One CSR stated that "the team leads are cool. They help you out. They make it fun and show you respect," while another one indicated, "this is a good and encouraging environment, with lots of happy faces. We like the help and support we get. There are lots of resources to help." Another CSR commented:

People want to do a good job, but are not given the support to do it. When you don't hit your numbers, it seems like the team leaders avoid you. They don't care when you need help. There is an exclusive focus on the numbers. It is as though every time a team leader speaks with you, there are strings attached.

A few supervisors who participated in the focus groups recognized the importance they had in motivating their workers. One supervisor remarked:

> *The number-one reason we lose people is the rep's experience of a lack of success. Everyone wants to have a sense of accomplishment—a sense that they are doing a good job. And we are not helping reps have this feeling. To the contrary, we are setting them up for failure. The ones who get support will be okay. The ones who do not get support and feel overwhelmed by the job—who feel they can't master the job—get very stressed and tend to have attendance and performance issues.*

This case began with several mysteries. First, the company was consistently and differentially eliminating poor performers every month, yet showed no improvement in performance over time. The chronic lack of performance improvement appeared to be due to the constant changes in products, services, and pricing that the CSRs had to promote. Many CSRs felt they could never do well and that they received little help from the company. The results of the survey and focus groups showed their ongoing training was limited, and their reference tools and leadership support did not fill this void. Further, CSRs felt they operated under the constant threat of being placed in the improvement program that they viewed as punitive rather than helpful remediation. They felt that many supervisors were unsupportive and did not help the CSRs deal with their situations.

The second mystery was that increased team performance was related both to the longer service of the team and also to higher turnover. From further analysis and the focus groups, it was found that supervisors were often placed in a difficult and unintended place. One of the performance metrics used to measure supervisors' effectiveness was the percentage of their team that met the sales goals. The explicit intention was to focus supervisors on improving their employees' performance. Unfortunately, most supervisors learned that it was easier, and to the short-term benefit of their own performance rating, to terminate those workers who were failing to meet their numbers before the end of the month, thus increasing the percentage of their team members meeting goals. This was often done without regard to the CSRs' past performance. It appeared few managers had the commitment to retain CSRs for the long term and improve outcomes.

A small number of experienced supervisors kept workers on, training and guiding them to improve their performance. While these supervisors paid for their development efforts in the short run, with lower performance ratings on their monthly evaluations, they built teams that grew in experience and skills over time, subsequently increasing the bonuses for both successful team members and the supervisor and adding to the company's bottom line.

Corporate culture also played a role in influencing the supervisors' behavior. From the results of the survey, it became clear that only one work location among many supported a positive approach to management. Not surprisingly, CSRs at one positive management site felt they benefited from the improvement program, but CSRs in all other sites viewed the program negatively. Another illustration of this site's approach to positive management was the fact that managers allowed team members to co-locate and support one another—a key structural component of the work design that was missing at other locations. For example, the research indicated that the return on the investment in extra and occasionally unused workstations paid handsome returns. The other locations assigned CSRs workstations as they checked in, so workers' locations from day to day were random.

By avoiding the cost of the extra workstations required to allow the teams to sit together in a stable location, the teams lost the value-added productivity that came with co-location and the ability to learn from one another. At all these sites, the workers had no actual relationship with their team members, and the only interaction with their supervisor was when he or she would listen in to their calls and correct them.

Define action steps to implement the solution

This case shows that an employee's commitment to her job derives from her experiences interacting with leaders through the filter of her own motivation and needs. An essential point to understand from this case is that while performance metrics are important, understanding what drives workers to achieve or to fail on those metrics is even more important. Without that understanding, performance measures can be harmful and counterproductive.

The findings of this analysis led to basic changes in how CORP managed human capital. It designed training to increase the capabilities of all levels of management with respect to assessing, training, coaching, and developing employees. It emphasized using performance measures for both CSRs and supervisors to improve performance. It determined rewards not just on a monthly basis, but on a long-term view of individual and team performance. It upgraded and improved the tools that assisted the CSRs.

Many managers could not make the transition to positive management strategies. Even after receiving training in how to manage more effectively, they simply did not want to perform those activities or found themselves unable to develop a supportive relationship with their workers. They were willing to track the performance of their workers, but were either not willing or not able to provide the necessary support to allow motivated workers to improve their performance.

There are two additional points to make about this case. Evaluating the performance of supervisors based simply on their ability to increase their team members' length of service would be a mistake. Unfortunately, making this goal explicit would lead supervisors to simply retain workers longer who were not performing and ignore the difficult work of fulfilling the management obligations of the social contract—objectively and fairly observing the performance of their workers, encouraging good work, and providing their workers with appropriate tools and assistance to improve their performance. The positive effect of the team's increased length of service resulted from the effort of their supervisors to develop, reward, and retain their good workers.

The second, less obvious point is that our initial analysis estimated an increase in sales of as much as $100,000 for every month of increase in the average tenure of the teams. This is a statistical estimate, highly influenced by outliers, such as exceptional supervisors with great skill and ability to manage effectively. The supervisors had worked for a long time to develop their teams, often bucking their immediate managers. The level of commitment of these outlying managers may have exaggerated the effect on productivity by increasing the average tenure of the teams. Giving typical supervisors the skills to manage their teams more effectively will undoubtedly pay off for the company but may result in somewhat less spectacular returns. Yet, even if only half of the potential is achieved, there is solid justification to invest in the improvement of the performance measurement systems, supervisory skills, the structure of the work, and the reference tools to support the CSRs.

Conclusion

In chapter 2, we looked at how companies derived great competitive advantage using analytics to design efficient processes and organizational structures and define the roles and capabilities of workers. In chapter 3, we looked at how companies achieved benefits from using analytics to build a talent supply chain or a pipeline to fill those roles. These two chapters use analytics to understand a somewhat abstract question: what would our profitability be if we restructure work and hire the right people to do that work?

This chapter dealt with the messier problems of understanding the dynamic interaction and exchange between the company and its existing workforce. It focused on understanding the strengths and weaknesses of the workers, their supervisors, and the environment in which they work. From the Sprint and CORP examples, we learned some important lessons about taking an analytic approach to understanding and improving workforce performance.

First is the importance of developing a detailed understanding of performance measures, both at an organizational and at an individual level. The interaction between various performance measures often has a significant impact on the behaviors of employees and managers, and often leads to a host of unintended consequences. The Sprint example demonstrates why it is important to not only measure performance but understand its causes and take action even under difficult circumstances. In the CORP situation, the need to drive team production led managers to make short-term decisions that were often in conflict with the long-term goals. In both cases, the difficulties associated with unclear and uncoordinated metrics led both organizations to make often detrimental choices regarding their workforce and had a negative impact on productivity and quality of service.

The two examples also highlight the variety of diagnostic tools at companies' disposal to get to the root cause of negative workforce productivity. In the first situation, Sprint was able to use data from its call-center management systems, as well as detailed observations and insights about the characteristics of high-performing call-center representatives, to ferret out issues associated with agent performance. The combination of competency-based models and performance data helped Sprint determine the underlying differences in service levels and quickly identify areas of improvement. CORP needed behaviorally based engagement surveys and focus groups to augment existing performance data and uncover the practices and the sentiments of a specific population of agents who were new to the company. The quantitative data added rigor to the analysis, while the results from the interviews and focus groups added color and impact to the discussions with key stakeholders. Both were valuable in motivating executives to take action.

Finally, each case focused on clearly framing distinct questions, rather than attempting to amass, cleanse, and mine huge sets of data that may or may not have relevance to the current situation. Too often, the proliferation of data across the organization makes it somewhat daunting to get at the heart of performance management questions. By setting up a series of hypotheses to test, both companies were able to target specific problems and courses of action, rather than being swamped by a deluge of data.

CHAPTER FIVE

Measuring the Value of Collaboration and Knowledge Capital

"The only irreplaceable capital an organization possesses is the knowledge and ability of its people. The productivity of that capital depends on how effectively people share their competence with those who can use it."

—Andrew Carnegie

In today's economy of ever-diminishing product life cycles and ever-increasing customer demand for new products and high-quality services at reasonable prices, innovation has become critical to the continued success and growth of an organization. The fortunes of Apple Inc. are a good example: when Steve Jobs, its main innovator, left the company in May 1985, its share price lagged well below $50 for years. Now, at the time of writing and some years after Jobs's return, Apple shares are close to $400, and it has consolidated its reputation as *the* innovator in personal computing, smart phones, and tablets. Its ability to take ideas, share them, improve on them, and execute is the stuff of corporate legend. Apple customers are some of the most loyal in history. Yet, despite the obvious value, measuring the return on investment of innovation and sharing of knowledge capital that drives the development of new products and services is seen as one of the most difficult activities to conduct and, therefore, to justify. The ability to develop and rapidly share insights around the globe has become an increasingly important element of competitive advantage, both in terms of the formal transfer of skills and capabilities and the informal sharing of knowledge capital, best practices, and expertise. As companies look to tap into the wealth of knowledge and expertise in their workforce, they have begun to invest in a range of efforts, from distributed learning systems to Web-based connected communities of practice, to online collaboration and advanced social networks. Some are even beginning to use three-dimensional Internet worlds.

However, supposed intangibles like innovation and knowledge capital and the sharing of these important organizational assets are often the first programs cut in challenging economic conditions. Companies struggle to address the key question, how can we evaluate and measure the value of innovation and knowledge capital and determine the return on investment? While many organizations have attempted to use various proxies to gauge the value, no reliable or widely accepted approach has fully emerged. Yet, we see signs that this will change dramatically over the next few years.

In this chapter, we focus on how organizations build a culture of innovation and measure the impact of these investments to adapt to changing competitive pressures. First, we will shed light on emerging techniques and technologies that are being used to increase the visibility of social networks, communities, and other initiatives and examine their effectiveness. Second, we will look at what companies are doing to measure the value of innovation and knowledge capital and rapidly disseminate this information throughout the organization. Finally, we will present two case studies of analytic approaches for measuring the return on investment of innovation supported by collaboration and knowledge sharing.

The first case study focuses on a European telecommunications company that put in place a state-of-the-art knowledge-sharing and learning platform for twenty thousand sales and contact-center staff to help them better compete in a suddenly deregulated business environment. The second study is about an Asian airline that developed a companywide approach to capturing and efficiently distributing critical learning, knowledge, and best practices. Both examples outline how to measure the value of knowledge sharing and development of innovation, using the six steps we have described in previous chapters.

Sharing Innovation and Knowledge Capital

The sharing of knowledge capital across the workforce has recently become a mission-critical activity for many organizations. The emphasis on developing and sharing knowledge capital has continued to increase as global competition and the rapidly changing financial environment have dictated the need to innovate constantly and effectively. Most of the companies in the services industry throughout the global economy rely almost solely on organizational knowledge, best practices, and proprietary methodologies to conduct business for customers. In fact, for many of these organizations, it is their institutional knowledge capital that helps differentiate them in the market and allows them to charge a premium for their services.

For example, a large, formerly state-owned European telecommunications company faced a situation in which it was under ever-increasing competitive and regulatory pressures. It had been privatized in the mid-1980s, yet enjoyed a monopoly until the late 1990s. However, things were about to change, drastically. With the commercialization of the Internet, the company was forced to rethink its products and services, and to transform from a traditional "poles and phone lines" telecom to a digital products and services provider. As a result, it faced the urgent need to convert twenty thousand sales and customer service employees from selling and servicing decades-old traditional communications products to selling Web-based products and services. This required innovation at the organizational level that went far beyond repurposing existing training and knowledge repositories for these employees. Internal surveys of the sales and service workers (including call centers) showed a woeful lack of basic understanding, let alone capability, to sell and service a rapidly emerging new generation of products and solutions. Fewer than 20 percent of respondents to the surveys had any experience or knowledge of what the Internet was or how it worked. How could they continue doing their old jobs of servicing their existing client base while learning new products and services and dealing with the disruption of change? Successful introduction of these new products and services required more than just the analysis and evaluation of the best form of knowledge sharing. Successful innovation required the analysis of:

- Which structures, processes, and roles would be needed to deliver the new products and services.

- What capabilities would the workforce need, and how to measure success and place the cost of transition into context.

- Which of the current employees would have the capability and interest in doing the new work.

- How to select and train those willing and capable, knowing that the processes and roles would change dynamically during the transition to a stable organization.

Once again, the challenge was how to quantify the effectiveness and value of disseminating key knowledge capital to make the case for what would be a very significant, but strategic investment. What type of tools and methods would be required, where to start, and how to structure and measure the benefits across a vast workforce were key questions that had to be answered. And in this case, the company needed to answer them quickly.

Similarly, there is the example from the highly competitive airline industry. In 2004, the CEO of a major Asian airline decided that one of his top-five strategic initiatives would be the creation of a companywide approach to capture and efficiently distribute critical learning, knowledge, and best practices, developed over many decades of business. The airline's business imperative was the rapidly changing demographics of the workforce, as it expected nearly 60 percent of its employees to retire during the next five years. Departing with these key personnel was the critical knowledge capital that had helped to build the airline into one of the world's best and most efficient. The airline is well known for its customer service capabilities, which allows it to charge a premium for its seats. The CEO's concern was that the top-rated customer service of the airline, and therefore its basic competitiveness, would suffer as the rapidly emerging, younger workforce would not be able to tap into all the best practices that the company had spent decades building. There were no methods or tools to capture these best practices and pass them on to the new generation of workers; and worse, there was no way to measure the value of doing so.

Clearly, the rapid loss of this knowledge capital would be potentially catastrophic to the customer service and operations of the airline for its immediate future and years to come. This situation came at a critical juncture when many airlines were under extreme cost pressures due to declining passenger revenue numbers after September 11, 2001, with many airlines going out of business. The first challenge was to quantify the value of capturing and sharing this knowledge to make the business case for the investment. Despite the obvious impact of not taking the initiative forward, the executive board, including the chairman, demanded that a credible case showing rapid return on investment be put in place and confirmed before funding was approved. The key questions were where to start and how to structure and measure the benefits. In addition, there was a question of how much formal knowledge capital would be required to support the new personnel versus more informal self-access, real-time knowledge and learning that would be needed across a dispersed and diverse workforce.

In both case studies, there was a critical business imperative, a need to define new approaches to innovation and knowledge sharing, both formal and informal, and a need to justify the significant investment required. This would necessitate defining how to measure the effectiveness and value of these assets in order to make the business case.

Using Social Networks to Measure Collaboration and Knowledge Sharing

Perhaps the most interesting recent development in the area of knowledge sharing has been the focus on informal social networks. For decades, sociologists and communication theorists have studied and analyzed social networks as a discipline to understand how individuals and groups interact with one another. Many of the tools and approaches that the disciplines in the academic world have used have now taken hold in the corporate environment. As organizations recognize the value of social capital as a key ingredient to sharing knowledge, they have begun to seek out and apply more analytic approaches to evaluating and visualizing these informal networks, tying them to business outcomes and using them to make human capital investments.

Social network analysis can help uncover a robust view of how work is actually accomplished, in contrast to traditional organization charts and process maps. It represents actual conversations that employees have day to day that enable them to do their jobs. It highlights individuals who, through specific knowledge or expertise or referent power, are the "go to" people, even though they may not have rank within a formal hierarchy. It can help to identify "brokers" who bridge functional or geographic barriers and bring disparate groups of individuals together, and "bottlenecks" who keep these groups apart. It can demonstrate how team performance is inhibited by poorly designed performance measures or a simple lack of understanding of the skills and expertise that lie elsewhere in the organization.

Social network analysis can take many different approaches in terms of collecting data. The more traditional approach to examining social networks is to survey a relevant group of practitioners and ask them to identify those individuals they talk to about specific topics or issues.[1] The surveys also ask the respondent to report the frequency of the interactions and whether the relationships are one way or reciprocal. Once the data is collected from people across the network, an analyst examines it and produces a series of metrics and maps that serve a range of purposes (see figure 5-1).

FIGURE 5-1

Picture of social network diagram and findings

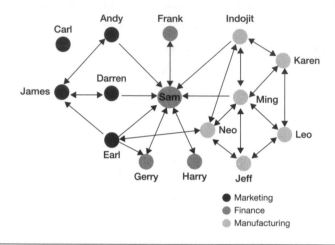

The maps help people visualize the interactions within the network and identify individuals or groups that appear to play important roles in the network (e.g., those that have a significant number of connections to others, a unique set of connections, or lack connections). From the diagrams, the analyst conducts follow-up interviews with key individuals to better understand the interaction patterns demonstrated by the diagrams.

At the same time, the analyst can produce specific metrics to compare different individuals within the network and better understand the interactions as a whole. Table 5-1 shows examples of some of the metrics that can be collected by conducting a social network analysis.

The metrics can then be used in conjunction with other performance-related measures, such as sales and customer satisfaction, to compare the effectiveness of different types of individuals and groups. Take, for example, sales teams at one *Fortune* 250 company.[2] The cross-functional teams were

TABLE 5-1

Actionable network metrics

Individual measures

In-degree centrality	The number of incoming ties a person has for a given relationship (such as communication or trust).
Out-degree centrality	The number of outgoing ties a person has for a given relationship (such as communication or trust).
Betweenness centrality	The extent to which a particular person lies "between" the various other people in the network. Networks that contain individuals with high betweenness are vulnerable to having information flows disrupted by power plays or key individuals leaving.
Closeness centrality	The extent to which a person lies at short distances to many other people in the network. On average, persons highly central with respect to closeness tend to hear information sooner than others.
Brokerage measures	We tend to focus on four measures here: people who broker connections within the same group (coordinators); those who broker connections between their own group and another (representatives and gatekeepers); and those who broker connections between two different groups (liaisons).

Group measures

Density	The number of individuals who have a given type of tie with each other, expressed as a percentage of the maximum possible.
Cohesion	The average of the shortest paths between every pair of people in the network.

Source: Rob Cross and Andrew Parker, *The Hidden Power of Social Networks* (Boston: Harvard Business School Press), 2004.

assigned to major accounts with a charter for growing sales and increasing customer satisfaction. When examining the social connections within high- versus low-performing teams, the company found that both categories heavily depended on two salespeople to handle the majority of communications with the client. However, in the more successful sales teams, there were many more supporting client relationships beyond the primary two salespeople. Essentially, the higher-performing teams made better contacts with individuals within their client organizations, which allowed them to more easily find out about new developments and priorities. Further, when the analysis looked at the internal relationships of the sales teams, higher-performing teams had greater reach inside the organization, enabling them to respond faster to client inquiries and bring expertise to serve the client needs (see figure 5-2).

Collecting survey data for a social network analysis can sometimes present challenges. For one, it is important that all the people who are asked to complete the survey actually participate to ensure that the survey captures all the relevant network connections; traditional random sampling techniques do not apply when collecting network data. Also, social network data is based on the perceptions of the respondent in terms of both the frequency and the quality of interactions with others. This can

FIGURE 5-2

High- and low-performing account team information flow

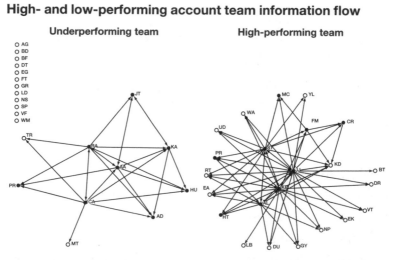

Source: Reprinted with permission from *California Management Review*, vol. 50, no. 4, summer 2008.

---

lead to respondent bias, with individuals potentially skewing the data.

Another approach to collecting and visualizing social network data is the mining of e-mail and other public and private sources. Software such as Lotus Atlas can collect data by scanning the content and outgoing addresses of employees' e-mails (for privacy reasons, companies typically allow their employees to voluntarily opt in to allow this data to be collected). Once the data is collected, the software enables people to view the social connections between others in the company, analyze the composition of their own personal networks, and find individuals who are working on similar issues. This capability empowers employees scattered around the world not only to find people with relevant knowledge, but also to identify individuals they know in common and can serve as references for them.

One recent study using social network data collected via e-mail mining reviewed both network and performance data, such as billable hours and revenue generated, from over a thousand IT consultants. The study found, for example, that individuals with strong links to a manager produced an average of $588 of revenue per month over the norm.[3] The study also highlighted that, while teams with strong connections to management can be valuable, having too many managers on a given project can actually be detrimental to project productivity. Overall, the results illustrate how taking a network-centric view of project performance and linking network data to outcome-related data can yield unique insights into both individual and group productivity.

This e-mail approach also has limitations. Clearly, the voluntary nature of participation can produce some bias that could potentially skew results. E-mail may only represent a subset of the actual communications that an individual has with others in the organization. People may be communicating with others on more sensitive topics or exchanging more tacit forms of knowledge through other interactions, such as meetings and other face-to-face conversations. Yet, despite these limitations, data-mining technologies can provide a useful insight into the connections and knowledge-sharing behaviors of individuals—a critical capability in a global, knowledge-intensive world.

Applying the Wisdom of the Collective Organization

In the previous section, we focused on understanding social networks, which primarily address the collaborative and knowledge-sharing activities of both individuals and teams. However, there is another level of collaboration that both taps into and leverages the expertise of the entire organization. Emerging technologies allow organizations to go beyond the metaphorical suggestion box to engage employees and others in the extended enterprise (i.e., suppliers, partners, customers) in an ongoing dialogue about the current and future challenges and opportunities. To effectively tap into the insights gained, organizations need to be able not only to collect this information, but to analyze the insights and determine patterns that reveal trends and directions that are actionable.

Two approaches address this need to tap into the wisdom of the corporation. The use of prediction markets captures employee input through a series of investment decisions. By expressing the insights as numeric choices, the organization can continually identify trends, reflecting daily or even hourly fluctuations in the decisions employees make to buy or sell positions in various markets. As James Surowiecki, author of *The Wisdom of Crowds*, states, "Decision markets are well suited to companies because they circumvent the problems that obstruct the flow of information at too many firms: political infighting, sycophancy, and a confusion of status with knowledge. The anonymity of the markets and the fact that they yield a relatively clear solution, while giving individuals an unmistakable incentive to uncover and act on good information means that their potential value is genuinely hard to overestimate."[4]

Another approach is the use of hosted online innovation events designed to tap into the richness of employee conversations. IBM has developed a process known as "jams" that are multiday online events designed to engage employees and other stakeholders in predetermined topics. In the past, IBM had hosted both internal events and events for clients on topics such as the company's values, the role of the manager, and the innovation process. Through the Internet, employees can post ideas, comment on insights posted by others, vote on proposals, and engage with people from around the globe. Not only do these events provide individuals at all levels of the company an opportunity to exchange ideas, but they actively involve senior executives as moderators to facilitate the conversation and obtain a firsthand view of what is occurring at the frontlines.

Analytics play two important roles in this process. One is in the management of the ongoing dialogue. During the event, metrics that highlight the location of participants, results from various online polls, and ideas that have received the greatest number of comments are collected on a real-time basis. These enable the event's moderators to focus on key topics and engage participants more effectively during the conversation. Also, analytics play a key role in studying the tens of thousands of responses that are posted during a multiday event. Even a sophisticated manual content analysis would have difficulty sifting through reams and reams of transcripts to identify key themes and translate them into actionable items. Instead, automated text analysis reviews all of the postings and culls out key patterns and trends that can be used to structure postevent follow-up. This is a critical capability because, without the ability to follow up on the ideas generated by the event, the investment in running a jam would be extremely difficult to justify.

Evaluating the Impact of Informal Collaboration and Knowledge Sharing

The challenge of taking an analytic approach to measure the effectiveness of formal learning programs is problematic, but perhaps even more difficult is evaluating the value and impact of informal collaboration and knowledge-sharing efforts. Over the last fifteen years, companies have increasingly recognized the need to collaborate, share, and, most importantly, apply the experiential knowledge and expertise that resides within organizations. In many ways, the most effective learning that occurs is informal in nature and takes place through a combination of on-the-job training coupled with informal discussions with colleagues, mentorship efforts, participation in voluntary communities of practice, and so on. Yet, having worked with many companies on developing and establishing these knowledge-sharing programs, we have found that identifying the hard-dollar amount associated with benefits of such efforts is elusive.

As companies attempt to quantify the impact of collaboration and knowledge-sharing programs, they have discovered many unique challenges:

- *It is difficult to attribute the benefits of collaboration and knowledge sharing to one particular group or department.*

Institutional knowledge often takes on the characteristics of what is commonly referred to in the world of economics as a "public good." Costs are often borne by one particular unit, while the benefits may be recognized by a completely different unit(s). Though one individual or group may invest in capturing the knowledge, transferring it into a format that is meaningful to some other audience, and communicating its availability, the benefits often accrue to other audiences that are evaluated on a completely different basis. For example, a set of leading practices developed by one business unit may have clear benefits to another business unit; yet, there is often no formal mechanism for tracking those benefits and directly allocating the benefit back to the originating unit.

- *Project success often depends on the number of people who participate in the activity.* Although the investment in an informal knowledge management program may be fixed, the true value of such a program may vary according to how many people apply their knowledge to a given situation. For example, the establishment and maintenance of a community of practice often involves the use of software to share documents, human intermediaries to connect individuals and moderate community activities, subscriptions to external content, and travel and expenses to support face-to-face interactions. While many of these costs have a fixed component, the success of the network is often based on having a critical mass of participants who are willing to swap insights, conduct training courses, and apply community learning to their particular jobs. For many knowledge-related projects, a critical mass of individuals is needed to ensure the meaning and vibrancy of the knowledge exchange before actual value is realized.

- *Benefits are often discontinuous in nature.* Unlike more traditional process improvement efforts, which often deliver a steady stream of results that can be consistently realized, the benefits of knowledge-sharing efforts are irregular and disproportionate in nature. For every five hundred interactions between members of a community or one thousand hits on a knowledge repository, only one or two might deliver a significant and measurable economic benefit. Yet, those individual interactions might provide contributions that far outweigh the original costs of the knowledge program.

- *Benefits are not always about direct savings, but measuring opportunity cost.* Often, many informal knowledge efforts are designed to save people time and effort in finding insight or recreating what may have already been done. Yet, capturing the value of time has often been the subject of much debate when it comes to making investment decisions. Finance professionals are often reluctant to recognize benefits that address "time saved"; rather, these metrics get pushed into an often ignored category of "soft benefits."

Despite these challenges, organizations have been able to define the business case for knowledge-sharing initiatives by tying their outcomes closely to traditional business metrics. Take, for example, the introduction of a mentoring program at Sun Microsystems (now part of Oracle Corporation).[5] To evaluate the success of this initiative, Sun divided employees into those who were involved in the mentoring program and those who were not. It then examined over sixty variables, including promotion rates, salary increases, and performance ratings to determine if there were correlations between those factors and program participation. It found, for example, that mentors benefited from the program as much as or more than the mentees did, that administrative employees benefited more than engineers, and low performers benefited much more than high performers. By establishing control groups, as well as tying the results to business outcomes, rather than simply employee perceptions, the program was able to establish traction within the enterprise.

Applying Analytics Through Collaboration and Knowledge Sharing at a Telecommunications Company

Let's examine in depth the case of the European telecommunications company we described earlier and the measurable benefits it achieved through the sharing of knowledge capital and innovation.

Frame the central problem

In 1999, fewer than 10 percent of this organization's sales and services staff felt comfortable discussing its new Internet-based products and services with customers. The company needed a new approach to address in a very short time the capabilities and knowledge-sharing requirements of a large sales and service workforce (twenty thousand people) dispersed over the entire country. The approach it selected was to "use the Internet, to upskill and share knowledge across the workforce *about* the Internet," as the managing director of sales put it. Because of the size of the workforce and the speed required, the organization could no longer rely on classroom-based role playing and static, paper-based knowledge repositories, which were the traditional, rather slow approaches used in the past to reach these audiences. Instead, the company developed a series of intranet-based customer sales and service simulation modules, supported by an online knowledge capital database, that allowed these critical field-based and contact center-based employees to practice realistic discussions with customers on Internet-based products and services from their PCs either at work or at home. In addition, as they were working, they could access a collaboration portal where they could rapidly find key nuggets of context-sensitive information to help them service customers in real time. The sales and service workers themselves—"agents helping agents"—put the knowledge there to collaborate on best practices. The cost to build and implement the tools and methods was substantial, and therefore the business case for the project needed to demonstrate not only the improvement in knowledge capital of the workforce but, more importantly, the increased *capabilities* of the workforce to successfully position and sell the new products and services.

Apply a conceptual model to guide the analysis

To construct and measure the business case with greater certainty, the HR leaders reached out to their finance colleagues to put together a pilot of the solution that utilized test and control groups to define the actual uplift in performance. They created a single simulation module combined with a collaboration portal with a number of basic-to-complex customer conversations, modeled from actual recorded conversations. They randomly selected four hundred employees from contact centers and from small- to medium-size enterprises to participate in the trial. Of these, they assigned two hundred to the test group and gave them the online, simulated, customer scenarios with collaboration tools, and had the other two hundred do traditional classroom role playing, based on the online simulation scenarios, with no collaboration tools.

The principles of the measurement model were to capture only the relevant data that could determine levels of sales improvement and customer satisfaction and the extent to which the learning and collaboration approach had an impact on them. The model was also designed to have a baseline of financial performance numbers for comparison. In other words, the company had a good idea of the base financials so that it could compare the data gathered and have a clear measurement of return on investment to justify expanding the pilot, should it prove successful. This model was the ultimate measurement of success.

Capture relevant data

The test group spent two hours in the online environment, while the control group participated in four hours of traditional face-to-face role playing. The company established a baseline of sales numbers, among other measures, for both groups. After both groups completed the learning events, the company tracked the sales and customer satisfaction numbers of the two groups every day for a month. The measurements included number of Internet-based products and services sold and number of up-sell opportunities identified, completed customer calls after the sales conversations, and total time on the phone or in meetings with customers. And for the test group, the company measured how many times the workers accessed simulation modules and collaboration tools after the learning event to see how often they used the tools to increase their capabilities as time passed and the original learning decayed. The project team executive board named a combined HR and finance team to pour

over the daily raw data and manually plug the relevant information into the model. In addition, the company trained sales and
service supervisors in capturing key data and observations to
support the analytics teams.

Apply analytical methods

The model and measurement approach proved to be very robust and created a clear delineation of performance between the
test and control groups. The combination of an analytics team and
floor supervisors, who could back up data with observations, was
very powerful in gaining the teams' agreement that the data was
accurate and relevant. The results were dramatic for all concerned. The test group achieved sales numbers that were 95 percent higher than the control group's numbers, and customer
satisfaction ratings that were twice the level of the control group's.
Furthermore, the test group was able to complete calls and/or
meetings with customers 23 percent faster than the control group,
with a higher quality outcome. In addition, the test group spent
half as much time in the learning event and twice as much time
using the collaboration tools and sharing best practices, compared
to control group colleagues (two hours versus four hours).

In this successful trial, the company achieved several objectives. First, the results could be extrapolated and a business case
drawn up based on actual performance tied to a financial ROI. Second, the company could use the same model to measure the
achievement of the business case and actual workforce productivity numbers over time. Because HR developed the model in conjunction with the finance department, the numbers were accepted
as valid results in improvement of productivity. The program went
on to be fully launched with a series of online simulations,
supported by online collaboration tools, for the twenty thousand
sales and service professionals and had the same dramatic impact

as the trial in changing the culture of the organization, while producing measurable ROI. The company achieved its goal: the upskilling and sharing of best practice across a vast workforce was a remarkable and, most importantly, a measurable success.

Present statistical findings to stakeholders

The key to moving forward with the full rollout of the program was stakeholder management. As mentioned earlier, there was a project executive board and an on-ground analytics team made up of HR and finance, as well as floor supervisors. The executive board consisted of the managing director of sales, the chief financial officer, and the chief human resource officer as well as leaders from marketing. The purpose of the board was fairly simple; it would make the final decisions on who to measure and how to measure the results, based on the results of the trial, and whether to fund the significant investment to roll out the full program and to what extent. Given the role of the board, it was kept abreast of the development of the measurement models and the implementation, and was also given a set of weekly metrics during the trial to assess progress. In the end, it proved crucial to have the board in place, to have regular readouts of the results and gain the board's buy-in that the data was relevant and accurate, and ultimately to predict that there would be a return on investment that was satisfactory.

Define action steps to implement the solution

Going forward, the company focused its main actions on efforts to scale the program and the measurement approach to all twenty thousand sales and service professionals, using the same model and governance. The team agreed to various "gating" activities, requiring certain success criteria, to be met for investment and the subsequent rollout to manage the investment and ROI and most effectively target the high-value audiences first for the solutions. The model was also tweaked as time went on, taking into account "bleeding" or corrupting of results from the more diverse test and control groups, as well as taking into account rapidly changing products and services. These actions were all approved by the executive board and were implemented successfully over eighteen months. The results of the full program were very similar to those found in the trial, and the program won numerous awards in the telecommunications company, as well as in the industry.

As we have seen, taking a structured approach to quantifying the benefits of sharing knowledge and innovation has a powerful impact on an organization's ability to transform how and what it sells to customers. In this case, the quantification made clear the business case for a significant investment, while at the same time defined the ongoing solution for continued measurement of the benefits. In addition, the approach created a cross-functional stakeholder executive board that not only fostered buy-in but facilitated a better understanding of how the organization uses its knowledge capital to improve business performance. The example clearly shows the underlying power of the six-step approach to transform how an organization operates and interacts with customers.

Applying Analytics to Disseminate Knowledge and Skills at an Asian Airline

Let's turn to the Asian airline described earlier in the chapter. In 2005, HR, together with the finance department, took an approach similar to that of the European telecommunications company. It developed a quantifiable business case for the relatively substantial investment to implement new technology and new methods and processes to capture and share organizational knowledge.

Frame the central problem

This airline's brand was internationally recognized as a premium international carrier, with award-winning service levels and prices to match. Its brand had been built from experience and capabilities developed over many decades, going back to the 1960s and 70s. Overall, many of the critical workers vital to continuing the premium service were getting close to retirement age (early fifties). The skills, knowledge, and capabilities they had built up over the years would be gone within two to three years.

The CEO made it a top priority to effectively capture and share these attributes with the emerging, younger workforce. In his mind, a failure to effectively pass on the knowledge, skills, and capabilities that were the intellectual capital of the company would be catastrophic to the airline's ability to maintain its premium brand and therefore premium prices. Unfortunately, the chairman did not entirely share the CEO's view and was more concerned about the estimated costs to implement the tools and processes required to address this issue. The chairman also questioned the value of the exercise, stating that he felt that the return on the investment would be little to nothing and would be difficult to measure accurately.

The solution first developed to address the problem focused on two main components: one, utilizing state-of-the-art collaboration and social networking tools to capture and disseminate knowledge capital critical to serving customers at the highest possible levels; and two, proposing a series of online and classroom-based learning events, where senior members of the workforce tutored the more junior members on the specific skills and capabilities they had learned over the years. For the purposes of the measurement model, a trial would be implemented only for the collaboration and social networking tools and processes, as these were the most expensive part of the program and the area in which it would be the most difficult to measure a return on investment.

Apply a conceptual model to guide the analysis

First, in order to target the most effective pilot project, the airline conducted a comprehensive analysis to understand which of the many workers that made up this complex global business would benefit most from having shared knowledge capital and organizational information at their fingertips. The analysis included extensive interviews (and on-the-job observations) of airline pilots, flight attendants, customer service agents, maintenance engineers, and ground staff. From these interviews and observations of key employees, a clear picture emerged of where access to best practices, product information, instant messaging, and other forms of networking could have a significant impact on productivity. In addition, key metrics started to emerge that indicated where the investment could reap the greatest rewards. To this end, a simple pilot was put together to identify the improvements in productivity and put a dollar value on these improvements.

As part of on-the-job observations, the team uncovered an interesting fact—the vast majority of senior flight attendants and airline pilots (both pivotal workforces) had purchased their own personal digital assistants (PDAs) and were using them to organize themselves for flights. None of the PDAs had access to the airline's systems at this point, but they could access the company's external Web site and other publicly available information (such as flight status). For the initial trial, the company gave several teams of flight attendants (the test group) Wi-Fi access to airline passenger systems on their PDAs. Instead of doing flight preparation in offices, they used their PDAs onboard the plane at the gate (Wi-Fi was already available onboard). Meanwhile, several other teams of flight attendants (the control group) performed traditional office- and paper-based flight preparations.

For example, flight attendants typically had to do many of their initial passenger preparations in offices at the airport. The preparations included determining the number of special assistance passengers and special meals, the number of infants, premium customer services, and other seat assignment issues. These preparatory efforts were key to smoothly running flights and required not only office space but a significant amount of time to go through paper-based reports. The premise and the value of the proposed technology and approaches were to reduce the need for office space (real estate) and decrease the time spent on preflight paper-based preparations, while improving the accuracy of data by sharing best practices.

Based on these observations, the company decided to conduct a trial for flight attendants and pilots. Similar to the European telecommunications company, the company adopted a test and control group approach in order to measure the effectiveness of access to collaboration and social networking tools in preparing for flights. A group of two hundred flight attendants and a hundred airline pilots were chosen to make up the test and control groups. Both groups had PDAs and access to publically available information, but in this case, one hundred flight attendants and fifty airline pilots would be put in the test group and given access to a set of new collaboration tools to help them leverage lessons learned and other organizational information to speed up their preparation for flights. Both the test and control groups also had access to the airline's airport and onboard Wi-Fi intranet and external systems for full connectivity.

Importantly, the measurement teams, known as the measurement boards, would be made up of HR, finance, and senior operations leaders, including IT technicians. As in the European telecommunications company example, the company created a baseline measurement of productivity for both the test and control groups, including:

- Length of time spent in airport office preparation

- Number and type of activities performed in airport office preparation

- Time spent in onboard preparation

- Number and type of activities performed in onboard preparation

- Customer satisfaction ratings of crew (flight attendants only)

- Number of access hits on the PDAs for flight-related information

- Accuracy and quality of flight operations (on-time departures, and so on)

The measurement boards were responsible for the development of spreadsheet tools to hold the data, as well as the observations required to capture the data. Board members participating in intercontinental flights had to make observations and take measurements both in the airports and onboard the aircraft.

Capture relevant data

Over three months, the productivity, including accuracy, of flight preparations was measured for both the test and control groups. This was a time-intensive and laborious effort requiring a significant commitment (and travel) by the measurement board members. They manually conducted observations, measuring specific data related to defined activities and keeping it in spreadsheets that they merged on a biweekly basis and consolidated into one repository for analysis by finance. The teams utilized networked laptops onboard aircraft and in the airport, leveraging the significant investment that had been made in Wi-Fi technology. The value to the organization and workforce of the access to these networks cannot be underestimated.

Apply analytical methods

As with the European telecommunications company, the airline observed an exponential improvement in productivity and accuracy (as well as savings on use of office space) for the test group versus the control group. When it compared the performance data for the test group with the baseline and the control group, the company found that the test group crews had a twofold improvement in productivity, spending half the time in flight preparations than the control group did. It also found that the test group rarely used airport offices for flight prep, preferring to use the networked PDA technology at hotels and onboard the aircraft. The flight attendants in the test group reported that they made extensive use of instant messaging and message boards to reach other attendants for advice and information. The test-group flight attendants also reported having more time available to focus on passengers and a greater ability to answer questions more accurately with the data at hand. Consequently, the airline recorded a 27 percent increase in customer satisfaction scores, relative to the control group. The finance department's analytics systems produced a dollar figure on improved productivity and cost savings that could be applied to the business case for this key workforce. The model defined two main areas of cost savings in the need for fewer flight attendants on some flights and the elimination of very expensive office space in airports around the world.

Present statistical findings to stakeholders

The measurement board presented the findings and the projected return on investment to the somewhat surprised chairman and the board of directors, and secured the investment for the full program of collaboration and social networking tools and processes and the learning programs that would be required. The CEO was ecstatic that this critical but difficult-to-measure human capital issue was being resolved, particularly during a very challenging time for premium carriers. The emergence of more low-budget carriers was making it harder to compete on a premium basis. The results and the approval of the investment came just in time.

Define action steps to implement the solution

Going forward, the airline focused on efforts to scale the program and the measurement approach to all twelve thousand customer-facing service professionals, using the same model and governance. As with the European telecommunications company, the team agreed to various "gating" activities to the investment and the subsequent rollout, first, to manage the investment and ROI and, second, to most effectively target the high-value audiences for the solutions. The model was also tweaked over time, taking into account the bleeding of results from the more diverse test and control groups and rapidly changing products and services. The measurement board approved these actions, which were implemented successfully over twelve months. The results of the full program were very similar to those found in the trial and continued to show superb return on investment, including payback of less than six months, in many aspects of the program.

As we have seen, taking a structured approach to quantifying the benefits of sharing knowledge and innovation has a powerful impact on an organization's ability to address overwhelming business challenges that could render it incapable of preserving and improving its market position. The quantification made clear the business case for a significant investment, while at the same time defining the solution for continuing measurement of the benefits. The approach also created a clear set of data and an approach to get a skeptical chairman onboard for a strategic business program in which the benefits were not immediately obvious. This example clearly shows the underlying power of the six-step approach to transform how an organization operates and improves its ability to perform at historically high levels, while preserving the methods and knowledge capital developed over many years for a new generation of workers.

Conclusion

The key point to glean from both these cases is that the traditional view that you cannot measure innovation and knowledge capital and its impact on productivity (and costs) is turned on its head. HR, working with the finance department, can develop analytics needed to quantify a business case. While rare, this is a powerful combination for addressing the need to evaluate learning initiatives. In the end, the mind-set of both the HR and finance departments needs to change in order to challenge the assumption that so-called "soft" benefits of human capital interventions cannot be measured.

As we have outlined in this chapter, there are many misconceptions, misunderstandings, and generally accepted principles that have, for years, created a mind-set in which most organizations assume that they cannot quantify the value of learning and knowledge. In addition, we have outlined approaches for evaluating the value and impact of more informal collaboration and knowledge-sharing efforts. We hope we have shown that, far from being "soft" contributors to an organization's value, learning and knowledge sharing are key to overall productivity and effectiveness and therefore have a direct impact on profitability and shareholder value.

CHAPTER SIX

Solving the Turnover Mystery

An Extended Look at the Workforce Analytics Process

"In the scouts' view, you found a big league ballplayer by driving sixty thousand miles, staying in a hundred crappy motels, and eating god knows how many meals at Denny's all so you could watch 200 high school and college baseball games inside of four months, 199 of which were completely meaningless to you . . . Billy [Beane] had his own idea about where to find major league baseball players: inside Paul's computer."

—Michael Lewis, *Moneyball*

T he chief information officer of PHARMA, a multinational life sciences company, discovered that several key IT initiatives intended to transform the company into a globally managed and highly efficient organization were in trouble. The projects were designed to facilitate the company's global integration through the development of rationalized finance and supply chain functions. This would give the company essential visibility and control that cut across national and organizational boundaries. The systems being implemented were not only new to the company, but also new to the industry, and required a change in the company's basic IT infrastructure and backbone. Overall, these projects were seen as critical, not only to managing the company's operating costs, but also to give the company greater flexibility as it expanded into new markets.

The IT leadership team noted that it was losing key people who were central to the success of the IT projects and the continued operation of the legacy systems during the transition. Some exit interviews suggested that people were leaving for large increases in pay. The compensation department confirmed that the salaries paid by the IT division were, in fact, $5,000 to $9,000 a year below competitors, but historically the company's generous bonus and stock option plans had mitigated these salary discrepancies. The CIO faced an important question: what was the root cause of these key players leaving at a critical juncture in the company's history?

We have described four important areas in which analytics can help organizations make more effective decisions that tailor the workforce to the demands of their business strategy: (1) developing a business model, (2) balancing talent supply and demand, (3) managing performance, and (4) capitalizing on innovation. Up to now, we have used examples of workforce analytics to highlight each of these separate areas. In reality, when companies face a challenge in any one of the areas, there are implications for changes in others as well.

In this chapter, we present an extended case study as an overview of the capacity of the analytics process to explore the web of relationships that affect workforce dynamics. The results of the analysis saved the company tens of millions of dollars and enabled the timely completion of a global transformation designed to make it more competitive. Analytics makes it possible to clarify relationships and evolve strategies and interventions that lead to effective solutions. The case example illustrates how a problem with retention can relate to a number of different issues, including talent supply, career management, employee engagement, and buried conflicts in organizational policies and structures. The case also illustrates that even within the constraints of a tight time frame, an analytical approach can point to immediate solutions and serve as a catalyst for building valuable infrastructure that moves managers from reacting to problems to anticipating them.

In the case of PHARMA, the need for a data-driven solution for an immediate business crisis that demanded a fast solution is often typical. Like many executives, the CIO needed this problem solved quickly to enable him to deliver on the IT transformation. His response to the initial assessment was to suggest a large pay increase for all IT professionals (about two thousand individuals) at a total cost of approximately $10 million to $20 million a year. He also recommended that the recruitment and hiring practices be revamped to improve selection and early retention. Executives in both finance and human resources recommended undertaking a more thorough analysis before committing the company to spending more than $50 million to $100 million over the next five years. With urgency, the CIO commissioned a team of internal and external consultants to do a thorough examination and find a solution.

Step 1: Frame the Central Problem

As a result of the company's budgeting and investment cycle, the analysis team had less than five weeks from the start of the project to examine the company's initial termination analysis, gather and organize relevant data, conduct the analysis, and present the results to IT leadership through presentations and focus groups. Such short time frames are not uncommon when analytics is employed to solve a pressing business problem. The analysis team began by obtaining pertinent documents and interviewing key players in the IT and HR divisions to gain a more thorough understanding of the company's immediate situation. It was clear that the company was growing rapidly after a period of stasis and that the new IT transformation projects were a critical part of the company's growth strategy. While the new IT systems were being developed primarily by a third party, PHARMA personnel were playing an essential role in the system design. Their knowledge of the company's existing processes was vital to the effective transition and implementation of the new system. To put the CIO's proposed salary increase of $10 million to $20 million in perspective, the expected benefits of the overall transformation would be measured in hundreds of millions of dollars.

Initial interviews indicated that IT managers were competent, capable, and concerned. Their project plans, time lines, and staffing appeared sound. Their leadership activities seemed to focus on achieving clear objectives, delegating effectively, and holding people appropriately accountable. They did not appear prone to reactively changing direction, giving unclear guidance, or being punitive in their dealings with subordinates. In fact, they believed that employee development at all levels of the organization was encouraged.

The HR function appeared to be equally competent. Reviews of its recruitment and selection processes indicated they were consistent with good practice. The compensation and performance management program seemed well planned with respect to the mix of base, bonus, stock options, and 401(k) contributions.

Their approach to career paths and compensation was not bureaucratic and allowed managers flexibility in acknowledging employees' growth needs. The company's recent success had made the stock option component of compensation very valuable.

There were, of course, the normal problems associated with any large project, but interviews with IT and HR managers failed to point toward any systemic cause for turnover. Overall, this division appeared to be just the right place for any ambitious IT professional, an area where new technology was being applied to projects designed to have a direct impact on the company's success. Despite the positive findings, there was consensus among all the stakeholders that key people critical to the daily operation of the company were leaving and only an inquiry based on objective data would shed light on the problem.

Step 2: Apply a Conceptual Model to Guide the Analysis

Companies today often house a wealth of data in multiple systems; unfortunately, this wealth of data often camouflages a poverty of information. PHARMA's process of identifying and pursuing relevant data had to be guided by a conceptual model that identified the metrics most likely to shed light on the drivers of turnover. Without such an approach, the analysis could be stumbling through caves of data for a very long time without knowing where to shine the light. Based on logic, business knowledge, and published social science research, a conceptual model outlines a set of constructs that is likely to predict a particular outcome. The analytics team identified a number of factors that are often associated with undesirable levels of turnover. These factors formed the basis for the conceptual model used to guide the data collection and analysis:

1. The jobs and the work may be poorly designed.

2. Planning and workload may be inappropriate.

3. Workers may be inadequately screened and selected.

4. Career development and training may be limited.

5. Leadership may be ineffective.

6. Workers may be dissatisfied with the tangible and intangible rewards they receive.

7. Organizational culture may not support good performance.

How these factors are associated with turnover is presented in table 6-1, which lists the primary underlying causes of turnover, the impact of each issue on workers, and the patterns of turnover generally associated with the issue. These hypotheses help interpret the results of the analysis. Some patterns are easier to identify than others. For instance, high rates of turnover in the first year after hire suggest that something in the recruitment, screening, and selection process is off track. Analyzing the relationship between turnover and compensation features (base pay, pay raises, stock options and bonuses, and performance evaluation) can clarify the actual impact of the company's financial rewards system. Turnover that is associated with particular job assignments, job titles, training, or promotion history illuminates the effects of career paths and career development on retention. Often, however, the relationships are more complex and the result of multiple factors, and

TABLE 6-1

Patterns of turnover

Underlying issue	Impact on workforce	Associated patterns of turnover
1. The jobs and/or the work are poorly designed.	• Workers are unclear about roles and expectations; teams are uncoordinated, with members often at cross-purposes. • Impact on productivity, overtime usage, customer satisfaction, sales, costs, etc.	• High turnover apparent in first two years of employment. • Sudden increase in turnover after a reorganization.
2. Planning and workload are inappropriate.	• Workers are expected to maintain unsustainable workloads; they may experience unrealistic time frames, constantly changing priorities. • Impact on productivity, overtime usage, customer satisfaction, costs, etc.	• Significant turnover associated with particular projects, particular managers, or particular functional units.
3. Workers are inadequately screened and selected for hire.	• The company and/or employees find a mismatch between worker capabilities or interests and work requirements.	• High turnover rate in the first year of employment as new hires leave the hiring unit.
4. Career development and training is limited.	• Workers rarely have formal training; company does not support obtaining advanced credentials. • No opportunities to develop significant capabilities through mentoring or shadowing. • Few assignments that allow employees to acquire new skills or demonstrate their range of skills. • Career paths are limited, unclear, or uncertain.	• Turnover is often apparent after three to six years of service, when employees see diminishing growth opportunities. • Turnover may be specific to certain managers, certain divisions, certain positions, or pervasive throughout the company.

(Continued)

TABLE 6-1 (Continued)

Patterns of turnover

Underlying issue	Impact on workforce	Associated patterns of turnover
5. Leadership is ineffective.	• Employees experience unclear expectations; shifting priorities, little accountability. • Little mentoring of careers by manager. • Rewards are not seen by employees as fair and merit-based.	• Clear variations in turnover rates across managers or across business units. • Clear variation in individual performance ratings as employees move from one manager to another or one business unit to another.
6. Workers are dissatisfied with their tangible and intangible rewards.	• Workers feel salaries are not commensurate with effort. • Workers feel their performance is not fairly evaluated. • Additional compensation features, e.g., bonuses, stock options, 401(k)s, are not widely available or are inadequate. • Workers feel they are not recognized for the growth in their skills and responsibilities.	• Turnover is associated with ineffective compensation features, particularly likely after first three to five years of employment. • Turnover is associated with lack of opportunities for career advancement.
7. Organizational culture is not supportive of employee commitment and productivity.	• Employees have little commitment to company; low engagement with work unit. • Impact on productivity, customer satisfaction, costs, etc.	• Turnover is higher than benchmarks throughout the organization, particularly in first two to three years of service.

thus more difficult to tease out. Problems with poor work design and poor planning, as well as with leadership, may be indicated by a combination of metrics that reflect productivity, performance, customer satisfaction, costs, absenteeism, and worker engagement, each contributing to a high turnover outcome.

Step 3: Capture Relevant Data

Having identified the potential patterns of turnover and their causes, the analytics team was ready to pursue its concept-based shopping list of desired data. It defined the appropriate analysis time frame as the three years prior to the current turnover problem. This minimum history would allow identification of trends and variations in patterns over time. Much of the five-week time frame available for this analysis project was consumed by the scramble to gather and clean the data.

Despite the storehouse of data in the systems that generate reports for HR, finance, sales, operations, purchasing, and so on, companies rarely have data that can be easily and quickly integrated across systems to answer meaningful questions about the management of their human capital. In appendix B, tables B-1 and B-2 list individual-level and organizational-level data relevant to workforce analysis. The tables show the multiple systems and subsystems throughout a company that usually house this data. Those systems are almost always maintained separately and independently from one another. Even data within a given administrative unit is often kept in multiple subsystems that are not integrated with each other. Because the various corporate functions have different responsibilities and diverse needs for information, much of the data across functions does not share common concepts, definitions, or time frames. This makes it difficult to build an integrated view of important dimensions, such as costs, performance, and productivity, by position and organizational unit.

Collecting the desired data presented the PHARMA team with a number of challenges that are common to the workforce analytics process:

- PHARMA had been through multiple reorganizations over the past three years, making it difficult to track organizational hierarchies and reporting relationships over time.

- There were no standard definitions of job roles and responsibilities.

- Little data existed on project assignments.

- There was no catalog of employee capabilities or tracking of completed training.

- Managers did not systematically employ administrative promotion codes. Therefore, promotion indicators had to be constructed based on a change in job title accompanied by a pay increase.

- Due to confidentiality concerns, yearly climate surveys, with potentially rich information, were only archived at the organization level, making it impossible to investigate variations in leadership across IT departments that might have resulted in varying turnover rates.

In addition to pursuing data from the normal administrative transaction systems, it is sometimes important to capture data through well-designed surveys and focus groups. Such data often provides the best metrics to assess the effectiveness of leadership in managing people and work planning and in creating an effective organizational culture. The goal is to build as robust a model as possible within budget and time constraints in order to understand the web of underlying problems *and* the interventions that will produce an effective solution.

In the limited time available, the analysis team could not access all the data that would have been useful to its investigation. However, the data it was able to obtain was more than adequate to convincingly delineate the problems. After significant data cleaning and validation, the following data on workers in the IT department over a three-year time frame was available:

- Assignment to the IT division or other divisions of the company

- Demographics (e.g., age, gender, ethnicity)

- Length of service with the company

- Job titles

- Performance ratings

- Base pay and bonuses

- Pay increases

- Stock and 401(k) eligibility

- Status—leaves, transfers, termination, including dates and reasons

Step 4: Apply Analytical Methods

With a clean set of data, the team used statistical and mathematical modeling techniques to explore the relationships between employee experiences in the IT division and turnover. To understand which of these different pieces of data were most relevant, the study team undertook a sequence of analytic approaches. Next is an overview of its analysis process, with illustrative presentations of its findings.

Applying Regression Analysis to PHARMA Data

Regression is a way of building an equation in which an outcome is seen as a function of one or more variables that appear to be highly correlated with it.[1] When the team applied regression modeling to the available data, it identified three factors that significantly influenced employee decisions to leave the IT department in any given year:

1. Their annual performance rating

2. Whether they had been promoted within the year

3. Their eligibility in the stock option program

These relationships are shown in figure 6-1. Performance evaluations were rated as low, medium, and high. Employees in both the low and the high rating categories were half as likely to leave as employees who received a medium rating. This

FIGURE 6-1

Effects of performance, promotion, and eligibility for stock on turnover

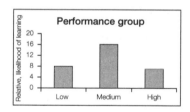

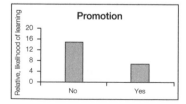

suggested that while the top performers may stay because they see a positive future with the firm, poor performers may not believe they have many other opportunities outside the company. Receiving a promotion (defined as a change in job title and an increase in pay) had the greatest effect on turnover, reducing the likelihood of a person leaving by 60 percent, from 15 percent to 6 percent. Further analysis showed the size of the pay increase did not have to be large to have this effect. Finally, eligibility for stock options more modestly reduced the likelihood of an employee leaving from 12 percent to 8 percent. The use of a pay increase, which would have been the most costly to implement, had no impact.

Applying Stochastic Modeling

The analytics team expanded its investigation by applying another set of tools called stochastic modeling.[2] Regression and stochastic modeling can, and often do, produce somewhat different results, but they can be used in a complementary manner to produce a much richer understanding of the dynamic processes affecting the workforce. Stochastic modeling can be used to directly observe the flow of workers through the company over time and examine employment events associated with that flow. While the mathematics can become very complicated as the impact of joint events are added into the predictions, you can see in figures 6-2 through 6-5 that the graphic presentations of how turnover occurs over time in relation to particular events can be immediately intuitive to the nonstatistician. Each graph illuminates a part of the story, and together they help identify not only what factors in the IT department were affecting workers' decisions to terminate, but how those factors changed over time.

LIMITATIONS OF REGRESSION

A regression equation represents the facts and builds estimates based on one point in time. Regression carries with it a way of assessing relationships that does not represent the dynamic nature of the processes affecting employees over time. For example, length of service, according to the regression model, did not even enter into the equation as a significant variable. But we know logically that time in the company will have some relationship to turnover. As length of service increases, there is a mutual process of refining the fit between the needs and expectations of the employee and those of the company. Each year, some employees choose to leave, and hopefully those employees who remain are the ones the company wants to keep.

At PHARMA, recent growth in the IT division meant there were many more employees in early years of service than

Figures 6-2 through 6-5 have the same basic format:

- The horizontal axis represents length-of-service (LOS) categories. These categories are in twelve-month increments for the first ten years, after which they are grouped in five-year intervals. These groupings include sufficiently large numbers of employees to reliably estimate the termination and transfer rates of the people in these categories.

- The vertical axis represents the percentage of people leaving the IT division from each LOS category, due to departures or transfer out of the IT division. While employees who transfer are not lost to the company, their services are unavailable those who continued over time. The normal process of work-force attrition reduces a large heterogeneous group of employees with varied interests and goals early in their careers to a much smaller, more homogeneous group later in their careers. Unfortunately, because of the small size of this important group with multiple years of service, the data did not influence the estimates of a regression equation as much as the large heterogeneous group with short lengths of service. The two groups will naturally have different expectations and goals and react differently to the company's incentives. The effect of overweighting in the large group can be adjusted for, but this adjustment further adds to the complexity of the regression equation and its interpretation. Logistic regression can give you the big picture, but the view needs to be refined to examine trends over time and whether there are effects on subpopulations. Small populations can have small effects in math, but large effects on the business.

for the IT division and thus affect the CIO's ability to deliver critical projects within the targeted time frames.

The rates shown in the graphs are smoothed and averaged over a three-year period. This helped eliminate random yearly variation and allowed stable patterns to emerge.

Figure 6-2 shows the overall pattern of turnover at PHARMA, with spikes occurring in three time periods: year two, years seven through nine, and years twenty-one on. Turnover in the initial years generally indicates a typical sorting-out process, wherein employees who find they are not a good fit with the work often choose to leave or are terminated. Those in the twenty-one to twenty-five-year category may not have been willing to keep up

FIGURE 6-2

Turnover in the IT division

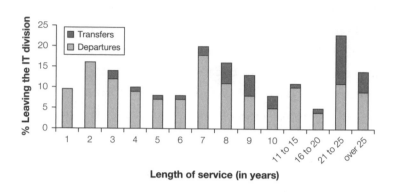

FIGURE 6-3

The effect of stock-option eligibility on turnover

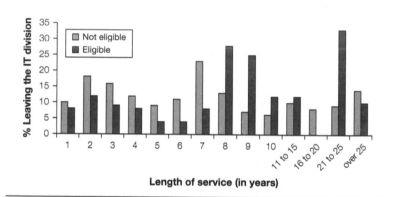

with the technical innovations required for the new systems; their transfer rate looks as if many were happy to find other roles in the company. It is the turnover in years seven through nine that begs further exploration, since these are typically "gateway" years when employees who have developed valuable knowledge and experience can expect to enjoy increasing authority and responsibility as part of a mutually productive relationship with their company.

FIGURE 6-4

The effect of salary changes on turnover

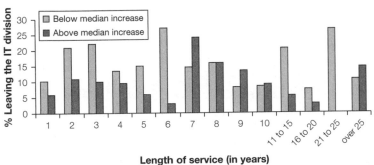

Length of service (in years)

What was causing the loss of gateway employees? The next logical area for examination was the reward structure of the IT division, including its compensation package and career advancement opportunities. Though salaries appeared to be $5,000 to $9,000 below those of competitors, PHARMA offered a competitive overall compensation package, including a generous 401(k) plan and valuable stock options for selected employees. The company's contribution to the 401(k) plan vested at the end of the fifth year of employment, and the spike in turnover apparent during years seven through nine makes it clear that the retention impact of this tool disappeared once the employee was vested.

Figures 6-3, 6-4, and 6-5 examine the relationship between turnover and stock options, salary changes, and promotions. Eligibility for stock options was conferred based on employee performance and/or pay grade. Stock options appear to exert some hold until the seventh year, but turnover continues to spike in years seven, eight, and twenty-one to twenty-five. Analysis showed that many employees who left the company in years seven and eight gave up unvested options worth many thousands of dollars.

FIGURE 6-5

The effect of promotion on turnover

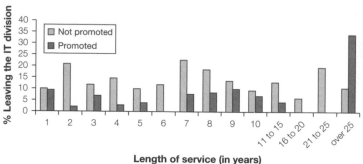

Length of service (in years)

In figure 6-4, we see that those who received pay increases that were above the median were more likely to stay in the early years of their employment, but once again in years seven through ten, those receiving larger pay increases were *more likely to leave* the IT division. These substantial stock options and raises were conferred upon employees whom the company judged to be valuable, and their loss to the IT division and to projects was undoubtedly disruptive. Nonetheless, substantial monetary rewards were insufficient to retain them.

The direct association of career growth with retention in the IT division is presented in figure 6-5. Promotion, here defined merely as a change in job title combined with a pay raise, has a much stronger effect than just receiving a pay raise. The graph shows that people in all but the longest LOS categories who were promoted were much more likely to stay. Still, there appeared to be a clear disconnect between employee rewards and behavior, so the team took a look at salary levels by length of service.

A simple analysis of the relationship of annual salary and length of service supplied critical new information. The employees in the six-year to nine-year categories had lower salaries than a substantial number of relatively new hires with lengths of service of one to two years. In presenting this analysis to the IT leadership, it became clear that in an effort to jumpstart the IT transformation and acquire people experienced in the new technology and implementation methods, management had gone outside the company to hire experienced, highly paid professionals for the last five years. Thus, these leadership positions were unavailable to internal employees, not even to those who had been promoted and well rewarded in the past. This action turned the opportunity structure on its ear by changing the career progression rules that gateway employees had come to expect.

The blocking of career opportunities was a completely unintended consequence. The CIO did not anticipate the effect on his employees of closing off key positions. He simply knew that the division needed skills that were not adequately available in his workforce. An ironic outcome of this solution was that projects suffered disruptions that could have been avoided with effective workforce planning.

Step 5: Present Statistical Findings to Stakeholders

Presenting analytical findings to stakeholders almost always provokes rich, focused discussions that simply do not occur without real data. In the initial discussions at PHARMA, the impact of personnel losses on projects meant that everyone felt pressure to take some quick, reparative action. There were few facts, only some ad hoc interviews with a couple of employees who had left, and a salary benchmark that showed base pay was low. The CIO's view of the problem was simple: people were leaving because of pay, and the obvious solution was to pay IT people more. In most instances when data is not available, initial formulations derive from hunches and often are driven by the need for a quick fix and/or the desire to defend certain programs or actions. With fact-based information in front of PHARMA managers, stakeholders became engaged in a deep conversation that led to genuine understanding and meaningful solutions for the issues affecting progress on the division's projects.

Addressing the Immediate Need

Focus groups are a useful way to breathe life into the statistics, validate the findings, and define and prepare the way for the changes the analysis points to. In this case, focus groups were held with both the heads of functional areas in the IT division and the project heads who were responsible for executing the transformation. Both groups endorsed the data indicating that advancement opportunities were going to outside hires, frustrating capable in-house IT professionals who had been performing well. Once the IT division leaders saw the analysis results, they had deep concern for the people who were at risk of leaving over the next two years. They learned from the data that 26 percent of their personnel were in, or near, the six- to ten-year LOS period marked by high turnover. If they did not take action to retain valuable employees in this group, the talent base of the company would continue to erode. In addition, the skill gaps that were plaguing project progress still had to be filled and in a manner that did not exacerbate the career progression problem.

Uncovering Additional Organizational Dysfunction

The focus group discussions also led to the discovery of additional problems with personnel assignments that could not be observed in the available data. Project heads were responsible for managing project budgets and time lines and acquired their personnel on an ad hoc basis by submitting requests to functional heads. Prior to the IT global transformation projects, this process had been satisfactory because most projects were less complex and of shorter duration. Under the current high demands for time and capabilities, however, the system wasn't working. During the focus groups, project heads complained about the churn of people assigned to their projects. They felt that key people were often pulled from their projects and arbitrarily reassigned. Project managers had no access to inventories of employee skills and experience and no authority to select or retain personnel on projects. They felt that department heads who "owned" the employees were unresponsive to their needs and, further, did not have the right inventory of skills to meet project requirements. The project heads felt that this internal churn in the division was as big a problem as terminations and transfers in causing delays to projects.

The functional heads had responsibility for the head-count budgets, staff utilization, performance evaluation, and career development of the people in their group, and the functional units were identified fiscally and culturally as the employee's "home." Since they were responsible for utilization as well as head count, they kept their staffs very lean. The functional heads confirmed their frequent shifting of employees from project to project. They viewed project assignments as temporary opportunities for employee development. If they felt that better opportunities opened up elsewhere or if the functional heads thought other projects needed more immediate help, they would unilaterally move an assigned employee to the better position. So, the IT leadership came face to face with the fact that assignments and job progression were not linked with the business needs of the company.

It became clear that the IT division faced human capital problems that went far beyond the initially identified problem of loss of key personnel on critical projects. To fulfill IT's mission, new policies and processes would need to be put in place, along with newly defined roles and actions to address the loss of talented midcareer employees, the churn of personnel across projects and functional units, the need for a robust human capital supply chain, and the need for more focused and effective employee training and development.

Analysis feedback sessions routinely provoke genuine engagement with the issues and provide new insights into the problems and solutions as managers interact with the data. The discussions in this case expanded the focus from the particulars of turnover among key players to the larger strategic problem of building and managing an inventory of IT professionals to meet the division's needs. The action steps described next, which emerged from the PHARMA focus groups, illustrate the convergence of perspective that can be supported by an analytical culture.

Step 6: Define Action Steps to Implement the Solution

PHARMA's IT and HR leadership jointly developed a set of action plans that covered a range of activities, from the immediately doable to those that required a longer-term commitment. A unifying factor was the new clarity about the business benefits of making the investments in management changes. The primary action steps included the following:

1. Keep the workforce focused and engaged to achieve business goals.

    • Identify talented employees at high risk for turnover and build an intervention program for managers to retain talented employees.

- Provide IT professionals with more control over their careers by:

  a. Formally defining career paths and development steps that match business needs.

  b. Publishing advancement opportunities beyond the immediate projects and work groups.

2. Realign the individuals, teams, and organizations with the company's strategy.

   - Build policies and decision structures to monitor and control employee churn within projects and functional units.

   - Maximize productivity by balancing head count, capabilities, and cost to meet the workloads of projects, not the utilization measures of department heads.

3. Build an effective human capital supply chain for the IT division.

   - Define key positions and their capability requirements.

   - Create a workforce inventory of demonstrated capabilities.

   - Project the types and amounts of work to be accomplished in a three-year time frame and match against supply and demand.

   - Evaluate risks in immediate hiring of new workers, contractors, or contingent workers and regularly reassess the best plan to meet the needs of the company and retain and build the in-house talent base.

- Develop targeted training opportunities for interested and talented employees, including mentoring where skill gaps are critical.

Lessons Learned

The results of the analysis feedback sessions at PHARMA reflect our experiences with other companies. While the particular human capital management problems vary from setting to setting, analysis feedback sessions routinely provoke genuine engagement with the issues and provide new insights into the problems and solutions as managers interact with real data. The clarity of outcomes that emerged from the PHARMA focus groups illustrates why companies that use workforce analytics to investigate a pressing problem move forward to build an analytical management culture. The organization continued to use and develop its analytic capability, which went beyond building a data warehouse and reporting tools. Each individual user had access to timely data he or she needed to make decisions on staffing projects and developing workers.

Managers in IT and HR wanted to move from reacting to problems to anticipating them. They saw value even in the hastily built analytical database constructed by the analytics team and felt that continuing to build on it would empower them to implement the necessary action steps. Making sure that new policies, procedures, roles, and actions actually produced the desired outcomes would require monitoring and effective information sharing and coordination across organizational boundaries. There were clearly identified stakeholder groups that needed regular access to particular information to be able to take effective action. Project managers, functional unit heads, and IT leadership would need to better share data on project staffing needs and project progress. IT leadership and HR would need to work together to better forecast future demand for specific roles and skills; better plan employee recruitment, training, and development; and formulate and execute more effective career planning. It was also recognized that HR should be an active partner in any decision to use third-party contractors. All of this communication would require efficient and effective ways of sharing data and monitoring progress over time.

CHAPTER SEVEN

Building a Sustainable Workforce Analytics Capability

"Companies increasingly have the ability to relate their investment in human capital to their returns on financial capital. Whether they have the desire, however, is another question. People may be 'our most important asset,' even our most expensive asset, but they are rarely our most measured asset."

—Thomas H. Davenport and Jeanne G. Harris, *Competing on Analytics*

M any of the examples discussed in chapters 2 through 6 represent specific initiatives companies have undertaken. The project teams collected unique sets of data, analyzed them with a small team of dedicated personnel, and made recommendations that matched the needs of the organization at a specific time. However, the projects were much like triage efforts in a hospital emergency room: they were short term and resource intensive, and only addressed issues that had reached the point where they attracted the attention of senior management. Like a high fever or chest pains, the problems were readily apparent (although their solutions were not) and had a clear need for resolution; a small group of specialists whose knowledge could be brought to bear on the specific issue could deal with the problem. However, as the value of these short-term projects became evident to the organization as a whole, the demand for such services often rose. In many cases, the individuals with experience in addressing the issues quickly became swamped by the many requests for assistance.

A small but increasing number of organizations have recognized the limitations associated with managing workforce analytics as a series of one-off projects and have begun to institutionalize their capabilities. Like a good preventative care system, a true analytic capability can begin to spot small problems before they become larger ones and develop recommendations to incorporate into the normal daily activities.

From our experiences in the organizations we have worked with, we have found that embedding workforce analytics into the fabric of a company requires the following important elements:

- *Data* that is timely, accurate, and crosses traditional organizational boundaries.

- *An analytic system* that captures, catalogs, and transforms the data into information that can be customized to meet the needs of different user groups.

- *Maintenance of the system* in light of changing organizational requirements and conditions.

- *Analytic staff* who can interpret the results of data and work with internal audiences to use the information most effectively to promote change within the organization.

- *Governance structures* that allow stakeholders from different functional and operational groups to voice their needs and prioritize enhancements.

Timely, Accurate Data

One of the most common expectations after the completion of a successful workforce analytics project is that building an ongoing analytic capability will be simple, since the initial project team has already collected the data. Often, this is not the reality at all. Many initial analytic efforts draw from databases that are basically static snapshots taken at a particular time. The data is often collected manually and reflects whatever is readily available to explore the company's problems and potential solutions within a given time frame. Frequently, the data contains flaws that, given the limited scope of the project, may not materially affect the outcome of the analysis. In most cases, strong relationships will not be masked or greatly exaggerated by small amounts of missing or inaccurate data.

However, to develop an ongoing analytics capability that a wider number of stakeholders can access almost always requires a much cleaner set of data from multiple systems. This requires dealing with errors in the source systems, such as missing information or poorly entered data, as well as harmonizing the meaning of data across systems. Data usually needs to be drawn from many different production environments that often do not contain standardized enterprisewide definitions of data elements. For example, labor costs defined one way in a manufacturing system may be defined somewhat differently within a payroll system.

A Customized Analytic System

During an initial analytics project, manually entered data is integrated with extracts from operational systems and captured for analysis in statistical packages not appropriate for use by a broad audience. Developing a more robust platform that can be used regularly by multiple stakeholders requires a technology platform that can:

- *Obtain data from a variety of source systems.* This includes extracting data from the source systems without interfering with their performance, and validating the data to eliminate errors and inconsistencies. These errors must be corrected in the source systems so that they do not continually appear every time the data is reloaded from the source system. Considerable effort must be made to harmonize the meaning of data collected for very different administrative purposes. For instance, finance will define business units and departments based on accounting principles and tax law, while operations will focus on how to control production and the supply chain, often cutting across financial boundaries.

- *Execute a variety of different analyses.* An effective analytics system has the capability to perform a range of analyses based on the information needs of the user and the problem at hand. For some basic problems, the creation of a simple frequency table or cross-tabulation may be sufficient to generate insights. However, for some problems, detailed segmentations, cluster analysis, and other more complicated statistical models will be required to guide decision making. An effective analytic system provides easy-to-use tools to perform each of these different tasks.

- *Present the information in a way that is meaningful and can be customized to different audiences.* Employees, first-line supervisors, managers, executives, and HR professionals all have different roles and therefore different needs for information. For example, a simple dashboard of key indicators may be sufficient for executives to understand if basic factors regarding labor costs, scheduling efficiency, safety metrics, and so on are falling within established parameters. HR analysts wanting to get underneath the actual data need to visualize more detailed findings using an easy-to-understand and predefined set of relationships. As we saw in chapter 5, visual diagrams to highlight informal social networks are one way that companies can obtain insight into how well collaboration is occurring and can provide a level of understanding difficult to achieve simply looking at numeric charts.

- *Deliver that information in a form that can be embedded within the business processes.* Many companies are happy to produce standard reports that analysts and executives can use to make decisions and justify actions. However, a more advanced way of using analytics involves incorporating metrics into the overall day-to-day activities of those responsible for the workforce. For example, if turnover within a specific group of employees reaches a certain level, an automatic alert is sent to the manager of the group indicating that he or she needs to take action to understand why this is occurring and how it should be addressed. Similarly, if there is a shortage of employees with a specific skill set, the system could then notify the manager that he or she needs to tap into pools of temporary workers or contractors for individuals with those capabilities.

- *Secure and protect the information.* Not only do analytical systems contain information about employees, they often contain very sensitive information regarding the company's business model and competitive strategies. For instance, one project that we worked on identified managers and departments that were at high risk for turnover. This information, if leaked to a competitor or accessed by someone without proper authorization, could have severe repercussions across the entire organization. Further, countries have varying privacy laws that can affect what data individuals can or cannot obtain for analytic purposes. All of these issues need to be addressed during the development of the analytical systems and processes. However, care must be taken in designing security for these types of analytic systems; a poor design can greatly affect their performance and response time and can be complex to maintain.

Separate stand-alone analytical systems may provide information about what is affecting the workforce, but taking action on this information by integrating it into the fabric of the company requires a broad range of skills. This includes expertise in extracting, validating, cleaning, and transforming the data from various source systems and loading it into data warehouses from which the information will be distributed. Data warehouse architecture skills are also needed to design how the data will be stored, distributed, and presented to the users. Individuals need to be well versed in database design and navigation, and knowledgeable about the tools to implement that design. Also required is the ability to conduct and record the design sessions, document how the system is built, build the content for the training sessions, and train users on the system. In addition to this core group of individuals, people knowledgeable in the source systems, data security, portal integration, and the daily operations of the business will need to be involved in the development of the system.

System Maintenance

After an analytical system is in place, dashboards and alerts developed, system documentation published, help screens defined, and the user community trained, changes that affect the ability to tap into analytics often occur. These originate from several places:

- *Changes in the source systems that feed the analytics* (e.g., new job codes, sales territories). Data from finance, marketing, sales, operations, and workforce systems is dynamic. Changes in markets drive sales divisions to create new territories, customer relationships, and sale incentives. Changes in tax law or corporate structures require finance to find new ways of allocating and accounting for the costs of organizations and work. Mergers, acquisitions, and divestitures will also continue to disrupt all aspects of the company. Improvements in technology force operations to reinvent how it defines the various components of manufacturing, distribution, and service delivery. As a consequence, any workforce analytic system will have to deal with new organization and reporting structures; new jobs, job families, and pay structures; new ways of defining an employee; and their associated costs. Trying to control these changes centrally will fail. As these changes will occur frequently, processes must be put into place to facilitate these changes and avoid disrupting the flow of information to people who rely on it.

- *Changes in the technology that delivers and integrates the information with the daily operations and processes of the company will be updated.* New hardware, middleware packages, and other technologies can have a significant impact on how analytic systems operate. These changes may affect how users get access to the systems, the speed of access to the information held in the systems, and the security required to protect the data.

- *Changes instituted by the users who become increasingly familiar with basic tools and capabilities.* As users become more familiar with the tools and the value they can realize from their analyses, there will be a continued push to update the tools as well as for new methods for analyzing and visualizing the data. For example, a company that has been able to successfully identify historical trends in labor costs will then look to develop models that predict future costs across a range of local labor markets.

In contrast to individuals who build analytic platforms, people who keep analytic systems operational on an ongoing basis require a different set of skills, rhythms, and time commitments. These people react to intermittent demands to correct data, respond to calls for help, update documentation, and conduct training sessions. They manage the ongoing communications and the communities needed to support end users. They collect and prioritize suggested improvements. They also manage relationships with the owners of the source systems that the analytical systems rely on to anticipate how those sources may change in the future. In addition, they have to stay in touch with the owners of the systems architecture through which the analytical information is delivered. The ability to manage these relationships with various groups of stakeholders is central.

Analytic Staff

As we have seen in the case studies throughout the book, the people needed to support the analytic needs of business leaders are often quite different from those found in conventional human resources departments. People working with business leaders on analytic problems must have mathematical or statistical skills and the capability to quickly identify and construct information from administrative data stores. They must have a deep understanding of the business and an appreciation of how the functions of HR can be mobilized to support the business. At the same time, they need to have knowledge of the change management implications associated with applying and sharing analytic approaches, including securing sponsorship for analytic efforts, obtaining necessary resources and data from various constituents, and gaining consensus and buy-in from those affected by the numbers.

As Greig Aitken, the head of human capital strategy at The Royal Bank of Scotland (which, despite the firm's recent financial difficulties, is well regarded for its innovative uses of workforce analytics) stated, "We don't talk about data—anyone can deliver a spreadsheet—it's all about insight, providing insight that enables more informed people decisions that solve business issues." To develop a human capital analytic capability within the organization, Aitken built a small team of human capital professionals from a variety of different functional areas. Most of them had worked in the lines of business as well as HR, with backgrounds ranging from finance, IT, to market research. This group not only had the capability to develop strategic models but could work with the business units to translate the findings into tangible actions for executives.

The team has taken responsibility for building a sophisticated capability to understand the drivers of workforce performance and enable managers to take action. One area where it has had a notable impact is in the consumer banking division.[1] By analyzing the results of customer service, financial measures, leadership scores, and other measures, executives identify those branch managers who play a significant role in contributing to the organization's financial performance. While not necessarily considered to be a high-profile job within the company, the branch manager position is, in fact, a "focal" job that has a direct impact on the profitability of the business unit.[2] By developing a clearer understanding of the drivers of successful performance for individuals within this role, the company targets its investments in talent management as a way of building competitive advantage in the marketplace.

The Royal Bank of Scotland found that there were significant differences in the leadership and engagement scores for the highest- and lowest-performing branches. This has led to a deeper exploration of the role of the branch manager, including the career development and performance management processes used to support these key professionals in the field. For example, every year, branch managers review the results of their branch's employee engagement scores with their immediate supervisors, the area managers. Before this meeting, the area managers work with representatives from the HR function to understand the results of the survey and produce a set of potential actions to address the engagement issues that emerged from the survey. Developing this insight before the branch and area managers meet allows efficient use of their time, but, more importantly, the meeting with HR gives the area manager time to work through the analysis with an expert on workforce behavior. This preparation provides area managers the knowledge to be effective leaders and coaches to their branch managers. By fully appreciating the contents of the survey, they are also in a better position to listen to and advise the branch managers.

In many of the other companies we researched, we found that professionals from outside the HR function often jump-start and lead analytic efforts. At Luxottica, Robin Wilson, the director of workforce analytics, had originally been part of the organization's legal department and had a background in process design and management from previous work at General Electric. At Qantas, the initial project leaders that Kevin Brown had recruited came from a variety of disciplines, including finance, audit, IT, and customer service, to build the skills necessary to develop and support an ongoing analytics capability. Companies such as Delta Air Lines and IBM use research staffs with advanced degrees in industrial and organizational psychology, statistics, mathematics, and social sciences. This is not to say that, within the HR organization, it is impossible to find individuals with the needed skills and capability to build a sustainable workforce analytics capability. However, most companies have found it valuable to draw on other functions or disciplines where analytic methods, tools, and mind-sets are more traditionally used, and allow these individuals to develop the subject-matter-expert knowledge relevant within HR to rapidly build their team.

For many companies starting out, the number and availability of individuals who have these critical skills and capabilities will often be limited. Therefore, many companies find it useful to house these individuals within a common department or shared services group where different operating units can use their talent. These central groups are often funded at a corporate level and serve as internal consultants to the business units. As the number of individuals and their capabilities continue to grow, they can be directly aligned or even embedded into the business units that they support.

Governance Structures

As in any complex, cross-functional effort, the ability to make decisions, allocate resources, and provide visible support is central to its success. Building and executing workforce analytic capability is no different. Clearly, we see the need for both individual sponsorship, as well as the ability to involve multiple groups of stakeholders in the overall decision-making process. Given the fact that workforce analytics involves resources and capabilities from various functional groups, such as finance, sales, operations, HR, and IT, as well as end users across the enterprise, a governing body that can evaluate the needs of various interests against the inevitable organizational constraints becomes important.

The Role of the Executive Sponsor

The executive sponsor is critical to the success of developing and maintaining analytic capability and the technology that supports it. For example, at The Royal Bank of Scotland, Neil Roden, the former group director of HR, played an important role in both communicating the importance of understanding the human performance dimension, committing resources, and bringing together stakeholders from different parts of the business. As Roden stated in a Harvard Business School case:

> It's a belief of mine that measurement is important and that in organizations you need to be able to demonstrate the value of

what you do. Because if you can't demonstrate that value, if you can't measure it, then you are in a difficult place if somebody says, "Well you want me to spend £500,000 on that, but you don't know what it's going to do . . . would you do that with your own money?"[3]

In many companies, taking an analytic approach to organizational issues is often a new way of doing business. In the past, managers and employees have not had access to this level of information and are not used to thinking analytically. As compelling as the initial business case may be in mobilizing cross-functional interest, organizational inertia can be profound. Choosing an executive with the vision, credibility, persistence, and communications skills to overcome this inertia is a critical hurdle.

Governance for a Larger Analytics Capability

A governance board is a small decision-making body made up of representatives from user communities, data suppliers, and technical staff. Part of its responsibility is to represent the needs and wishes of its separate constituencies. But equally essential are group members who focus objectively on the priorities of the business as a whole and the return on investment achieved by pursuing one option over another. The formation of three separate advisory groups that represent the users, information suppliers, and IT services may relieve the pressure to advocate for individual needs. Each should have input to the governance body so that it can more directly advocate for its needs but not be a part of the decision-making group.

The members of the group are the primary decision makers for the design and delivery of the analytics system. The governance group's composition is vitally important, although the selections are often based on politics and finances. Who has clout and who has the budget can mean that user groups with tight budgets, typically HR, are unduly restricted in their influence. It is essential that the power and money represented by any group member be secondary to a decision-making process with clearly stated principles by which the group chooses the initiative that supports the best interests of the company. The governance board should not approach decision making by saying, "Here is our budget. What can we do with it?" Instead, it must go the other way around: "What will benefit the company most and how can we pay for it?"

The governance board members should demonstrate three critical skills in addition to the expertise required by their jobs:

- *The desire to collaborate with people across a wide range of functional and professional boundaries.* This collaboration involves a willingness to learn what the people in the community are trying to achieve, what they need to do their jobs, and how to accommodate those needs. It requires an understanding of cause and effect and the interdependency of data and functions.

- *The willingness to serve multiple masters and deal with ambiguity.* Collaboration across functional boundaries means experiencing multiple demands, all of which have legitimacy within the perspective of their individual function. Key here is the willingness to multitask and deal with disruptions to their "day jobs" and the inherent conflict of serving the interests of the organization over the parochial interests of their function.

- *Vision and deep subject-matter expertise that allows the participants to execute their immediate jobs well and contribute effectively to the group.* This expertise should also give them the confidence to contribute in a forthright way, advocate for their position, as well as understand the perspectives of the group as a whole.

Key Questions in Building a Sustainable Analytics Capability

Senior executives at companies wanting to move beyond individual analytic projects and develop a more institutionalized workforce analytic capability should consider the following questions:

- Do I have the commitment of top management to pursue analytics within my organization?

- Have I established a governance process focused on the overall interests and needs of the company?

- Have I earned support by building a compelling business case and road map that demonstrates the benefit of using analytics to drive performance?

- Is my workforce data clean, consistent, and able to be integrated with data from other parts of the organization?

- Do I have a technology platform that allows me to perform various types of workforce analyses in a timely and accurate manner?

- Do I have the resources within my organization to build, maintain, and support an ongoing workforce analytic capability?

Through our work with senior executives in both large global companies and rapidly growing smaller ones, we have been encouraged to hear many of them talk about their aspirations to implement a robust approach to workforce analytics. They articulate a sense of urgency around the need for a new approach and the value of having deeper insights into their human capital. What we have tried to do in this book is to inspire senior executives to move from aspirations to action by providing both a framework and methods to achieve their goals.

We saw how a number of companies are using analytics to address common workforce-related challenges: for example, linking strategy and organization design, building effective human capital supply chains to match the right people to the right positions, and ensuring that once workers are in place they are focused and engaged in meeting company objectives. We also saw how innovations are identified, developed, and shared across the organization, demonstrating the intrinsic, measurable value workforce analytics creates. Companies like Royal Bank of Scotland, Delta Air Lines, IBM, and Sprint, among others, have galvanized their organizations behind this idea that a deeper insight into employees and their work is ultimately a deeper insight into what really makes the organization tick. We examined in detail the different technologies, processes, organizational structures, and staffing that are required to successfully develop—and most importantly—sustain an analytical culture.

We have said before that analytics is the connective tissue between vision and action—not an abstraction or a set of tools looking for a problem. That connective tissue, the sinew and muscle of an organization, must have a focus and a cause for action. Many of the companies we studied started with a small, well-defined problem. For example, one company focused on a retention problem that was threatening a key global transformation project. In analyzing this problem, senior executives uncovered the root cause of what turned out to be just a symptom. By understanding the cause, they were able to achieve much more than simply retaining talented people in a dysfunctional organization. The process of analysis and disciplined inquiry—even into a seemingly isolated problem—can lead to great insight and effective action.

We have journeyed through a number of organizations, from Qantas Airlines, which used scorecard analytics in a unique way to articulate its strategic goals and drive change, to Luxottica and IBM, where leaders translated the capabilities required for key positions into standards for recruiting, selecting, and deploying workers. The examples provided by Sprint and CORP revealed a number of important lessons about taking an analytic approach to understanding and improving workforce performance, as did a major Asian airline and a European telecommunications company's approach to developing, sharing, and measuring the value of knowledge capital to drive innovation and performance. In PHARMA, an IT division of a pharmaceutical company we worked with, we saw how both IT and HR managers wanted to move from reacting to problems to anticipating them. The clear results that emerged from their focus groups illustrate why companies that use workforce analytics to investigate problems move forward to build an analytical management culture.

As we have seen, there are substantial benefits to be gained by focusing on workforce analytics. It gives companies a powerful tool that allows them to create new ways to compete based on how they organize and deploy their workforces. Companies that use a focused and structured approach to workforce analytics develop a greater respect for, and understanding of, their employees, and they recognize the competitive advantage that a well-organized, highly skilled, and well-motivated workforce can produce.

Organizations face challenging times ahead, and attempting to navigate choppy waters and unseen hazards is never welcome, nor, as we have shown, is it necessary. Throughout our journey in researching and writing this book, we have seen a common thread emerge: there is more measurable value inside an organization than meets the eye—if it is sought out and quantified. Taking a structured approach—in this case our Six Step method—and combining it with the right expertise and sponsorship can unlock immense value.

The Components of a Behavioral Survey to Understand the Drivers of Workforce Engagement

1. How successful is the design of the work?
   Is it possible to do the job that workers are asked to do in the way they are asked to do it and are the processes efficient? Clearly, jobs that frustrate incumbents are destined to fail.

   - Are the objectives of selling products and services and resolving customer problems achievable? Are the prescribed sequences of behaviors the workers are expected to follow clearly defined and appropriate?

   - Is the work generally stable and predictable?

   - Do the working conditions interfere with their ability to do the work?

   - Do the tools used by workers provide the necessary support to help with customer relationship management and resolve customer issues?

2. How successful are the performance measurement and reward systems?
   Do workers believe their performance is measured fairly and rewarded equitably?

- Are the performance standards observable, measurable, objective, reliable, and appropriate to the job?

- Are the rewards consistent with the effort required and the expectations of the workers with regard to:

  - Tangible rewards, such as money, bonuses, and benefits.

  - Intangible rewards, such as skill development, advancement, and a sense of being respected and valued.

3. Does recruitment and selection produce appropriate job candidates?

   Is the selection process successful in hiring people who are capable of doing the job? Do the incumbents feel that they can do the job, and did the workers get the job they expected? Just as toxic as hiring workers who don't have the ability to succeed is hiring workers into jobs they are not interested in.

   - Did the prehire job description match the job the worker was given?

   - Do the job incumbents feel capable of doing the work and are they motivated to do it?

   - Are the workers' needs and expectations consistent with what the company can offer with respect to pay, benefits, skill development, advancement, professional challenge, security, company culture, and the balance between company demands and personal obligations?

   - Are workers capable of adapting to the working conditions, hours, and physical work environment?

- Are they willing and capable of learning and adapting to new job demands?

4. Is training and development being used to support workers' capacity to do the job?

Are workers given the training required to do their jobs and are their skills updated as the job requirements change? No matter how talented the new hires are, they must be taught what is expected of them and how to deliver it. Poor preparation, inadequate communication of changes in job requirements, and inadequate support tools can cause chaos, poor productivity, and feelings of inadequacy and anger.

- Did workers' post-hire training prepare them for the job?

- Is ongoing training available and appropriate?

- Are knowledge support tools available and effective in supporting work performance?

5. Is workforce planning effective in matching supply with demand and deploying people where they are needed?

Obviously, putting workers in a position where they may be overwhelmed with the volume of work or bored by the lack of it, or scheduled to work at times when what they are asked to do is not aligned with their abilities is frustrating. It is often difficult for workers to be regularly required to react to scheduling changes on short-term notice.

- Are schedules published well in advance?

- Are schedules designed with some flexibility for the workers?

- Are workloads stable and achievable?

- Is overtime controlled?

6. Are workers' important needs being met?

From the workers' point of view, this has two components. First, is the company delivering on its part of the
bargain?

- Are the tangible and intangible rewards consistent
  with the ones workers expected?

- Does the job allow them to succeed by using their
  skills, providing the tools and learning they require to
  succeed and defining clear measurable and achievable
  metrics?

Second, job commitment can be affected by forces outside the company's control. These factors include everything from the health of the workers to their obligations
to their families and communities. External demands
can, and will, affect the ability of and the commitment of
workers to do their job. Here, one is interested in the impact of:

- How do local labor market opportunities compare to
  an individual's current job?

- How is the job affected by family and community
  pressure?

- To what extent do commuting and traveling impact
  an individual's job perception?

- Are the rewards they are receiving the ones they now
  need, based on how the conditions of their lives may
  have changed?

7. Is leadership effective in motivating workers?

Within the constraints of the company culture, do the first-line supervisors motivate their workers to perform well? Even in the most narrow and oppressive cultures, effective leaders have some latitude to get the best from their people. Examining how individual supervisors use the tools they are given provides a wealth of knowledge in identifying and solving the organization's performance problems.

- Are managers making their expectations clear?

- Are they accurately and reliably observing workers' performance?

- Are managers willing to recognize problems and seek solutions?

- Do managers give effective feedback on performance and constructive suggestions on how to improve?

- Are individuals treated equitably?

- Do managers support their employees' growth?

8. Does the culture of the workplace community demonstrate and encourage behavior that is positive, supportive, consistent, and fair?

Culture is the ether through which the influence of everything described earlier is felt, and there is a direct relationship between company culture and company financial performance. The company's culture reflects the prevailing norms and values through a variety of signs and symbols in employees' daily interactions. The work can be demanding and performance measures challenging if the values of the company support and confirm the value of workers' efforts. However, even if the first seven dimensions are well designed, the effort placed into creating a well-conceived human capital approach will be overridden by an atmosphere that is demeaning, capricious, and/or arbitrary.

- Is the work environment supportive of employees' efforts?

- Are messages consistent and reinforcing from all levels of the company?

- Is there wide variation in treatment across location and supervisors?

- Is the environment stable or one that is constantly changing and is that change planned and controlled or reactive?

9. To what extent are employees engaged in their work?
This concept has a very broad range of indicators. If measured well, engagement is highly correlated with retention rates and productivity. The recommended measures are all behavioral and have a clear progression indicting the level of commitment:

- Is the worker actively engaged in planning his or her exit, looking for another job, or discouraging friends and coworkers from working for the company?

- Is the worker's attendance reliable?

- Is the worker doing at least the minimum required of the job?

- Is the worker actively looking for ways to improve his or her own and the team's performance?

- Is the work and the work environment fulfilling?

Sources of Data Relevant to Turnover Analysis

Sources of individual worker-level data relevant to turnover analysis

Employee	Source systems	Data
Prehire qualifications	• HR applicant tracking system	Prior to hire: Education, work history, licenses and certifications, professional training, language skills, hiring assessment scores
Demographics	• HR employee base system	Age, race, gender, address, citizenship, visas
Interests, aspirations, perceptions	• Talent management system • Succession planning system • Survey data	Career goals, availability for assignments, personal constraints, workplace evaluations, engagement
Organizational placement	• HR employee base system • Operations system • Finance system • Business unit system	Job, position, department, location, project assignments
Pay	• HR employee base system • HR payroll system	Pay grade, base pay, bonus, overtime, premium pay
Benefit and compensation plan participation	• HR compensation system • Benefits plan system • Savings plan system • Stock options system	Eligibility status, vesting dates, dollar values

(Continued)

Sources of individual worker-level data relevant to turnover analysis

Employee	Source systems	Data
Performance measures	• HR performance system • Business unit performance system	Performance evaluations, productivity measures, quality measures, customer satisfaction
Career development	• HR learning management system • Talent management system • Succession planning system • Business unit management system	Training courses, development activities, licenses and certifications, temporary assignments, project assignments
Capabilities	• HR skills inventory system • Business unit skills inventory system	Knowledge, skills, and abilities; relevant personality traits
Status	• HR employee base system • HR payroll system • Business unit organizational system	Hire, leave, transfer, termination dates
Cost	• HR employee base system • HR payroll system • HR benefits system • HR compensation plan system • Finance system	Total cost of employee: pay, benefits, additional compensation features, training

Contractor	Source systems	Data
Contract period	• Purchasing system • Business unit/project system	Start date, end date for contract position
Qualifications	• Business unit system	Requirements stipulated for each contract position: education, experience, licenses and certifications, language skills
Organizational placement	• Purchasing system • Business unit system	Job, position, location, project assignment
Cost	• Purchasing system • Business unit system	Total cost of individual contractor

TABLE B-2

Sources of organizational-level data relevant to turnover analysis

Business unit/ team level	Source systems	Data
Organizational structure	• HR reference tables • CRM and sales systems • Manufacturing systems • Project management systems • Organizational charting software • Climate surveys	• Position reporting structure • Position approval authority • Jobs associated with positions • Position status—active/inactive • Identification of key positions for projects/teams • Business unit budget/team budget • Location breakdowns
Planning and workload	• Labor supply and demand projections • Scheduling software • Scenario planning and optimization software • Manufacturing and supply chain software • Sales projections • Climate surveys	• Work standards • Staffing models • Project scheduling • Product scheduling • Labor costing models • Overtime policies • Work rules
Development and training	• Learning management systems • Succession planning • Project management • HR systems • Climate surveys	• Training and development opportunities, formal and informal • Course curricula • Career paths
Leadership	• Climate surveys • Performance evaluations • 360-degree evaluations	• Fairness, clarity of expectations, accountability, open communication, engagement, etc.

(Continued)

TABLE B-2 (Continued)

Sources of organizational-level data relevant to turnover analysis

Business unit/ team level	Source systems	Data
Reward structure	• Career development system • HR/compensation system • HR/payroll • Third-party systems for stock options, 401(k)s • Climate surveys	• Mentoring of career development of direct reports • Career structures • Salary structure • Compensation plan policies, eligibility, vesting, timing of events
Performance measures	• CRM and sales systems • Project management systems • Manufacturing systems • Supply chain systems • Finance systems • Payroll	• Productivity measures • Cost measures • Quality measures • Customer satisfaction measures • Profitability

Chapter 1

1. Robert Kaplan and David P. Norton, *The Balanced Scorecard* (Boston: Harvard Business School Press, 1996), 11.

2. Ibid.; Thomas H. Davenport and Jeanne Harris, *Competing on Analytics* (Boston: Harvard Business Press, 2007), 77–78; and Cascio and Boudreau, *Investing in People*, 2.

3. David Carr, "Thousands are Laid Off at Circuit City: What's New?" *New York Times*, April 2, 2007.

4. Thomas Kuhn, *The Structure of Scientific Revolution*, 3rd ed. (Chicago and London: University of Chicago Press, 1996).

5. Probably the most famous example of study effects is the work that was conducted at Western Electric's Hawthorne Works plant outside Chicago between 1924 and 1932. The reanalysis of the data showed that the improvement in performance was more a result of the measurement process than the actual intervention. See Henry A. Landsberger, *Hawthorne Revisited* (Ithaca, NY: Cornell University, 1958); and Elton Mayo, *Hawthorne and the Western Electric Company, The Social Problems of an Industrial Civilization* (London U.K.: Routledge, 1949).

6. John W. Boudreau, *Retooling HR* (Boston: Harvard Business School Press, 2010), 10.

Chapter 2

1. Andrew J. Bacevich, "The Petraeus Doctrine," *The Atlantic*, October 2008, www.theatlantic.com/magazine/archive/2008/10/the-petraeus-doctrine.

2. Robert S. Kaplan and David P. Norton, *The Balanced Scorecard* (Boston: Harvard Business School Press, 1996), 11.

3. Morten T. Hansen, *Collaboration* (Boston: Harvard Business Press, 2009).

4. Peter Cappelli, *Talent On Demand* (Boston: Harvard Business Press, 2008), 217.

Chapter 3

1. Parts of this chapter have been adapted, with permission, from articles that have been previously published by the *International Human Resources Information Management Journal*. These include: Eric Lesser and Vijay Mehotra, "Creating Value from Investments in Labor Scheduling," *IHIRM Journal*, May/June 2006; Carl Hoffmann and Kathleen Hoffmann, "HR Can Do Business! Delivering the Right Workforce," *IHIRM Journal*, September 2007; and Thomas Stachura and Eric Lesser, "Workforce Planning as Competitive Advantage: Enabling Success in a Services Business," *IHRIM.Link*, June/July 2008.

2. See Peter Cappelli, *Talent On Demand: Managing Talent in an Age of Uncertainty* (Boston: Harvard Business Press, 2008).

3. Nancy Weber and Lureen Patten, "Shoring Up for Efficiency," *Health Management Technology* 26, no. 1 (January 2005): 34–36.

4. Natalie Stevenson, "Metro Uses Workplace to Slash Labour Costs," *Retail Week*, June 17, 2005.

5. Bruce H. Andrews and Shawn M. Cunningham, "L.L. Bean Improves Its Call Forecasting," *Interfaces* 25, no. 6 (1995): 1–13; and Bruce H. Andrews and Henry Parsons, "Establishing Telephone Agent Staffing Levels Through Economic Valuation," *Interfaces* 23, no. 2 (1993): 14–20.

6. Cappelli, *Talent On Demand*, 141.

7. David Niles, "The Secret of Successful Scenario Planning," *Forbes*, August 3, 2009.

Chapter 4

1. For a more in-depth review of the literature in this area, see John Gibbons, "Employee Engagement: A Review of Current Research and Its Implications," Conference Board Report E-0010-06-RR, 2006.

2. Wayne Cascio and John Boudreau, *Investing in People: Financial Impact of Human Resource Initiatives* (Upper Saddle River, NJ: FT Press, 2008).

3. Given the sensitivity of the data, the company asked that both its name and industry be withheld. However, we believe its analysis and experience are relevant to call centers in a variety of industries, such as financial

services, telecommunications, information technology, travel and leisure, and retail.

4. The method used was stepwise linear regression. Regression is a way of understanding the relationship of one variable to another. Here we are interested in predicting the sales of the team based on specific characteristics of the teams. The level of sales became a function of those characteristics. There are statistical processes to test whether these relationships are nonrandom. Statistically, the relationships reported here could not have happened by chance more than one time in twenty. In most cases, we will stress the sign or direction of the relationship, either positive or negative, and the percentages of the variance explained by each significant variable. Here we also examine the estimate of that relationship. Regression does have its limits; see C. C. Hoffmann and D. Quade, "Regression and Discrimination: A Case of Lack of Fit," in *Sociological Methods and Research* (Beverly Hills, CA: Sage Publications, May 1983).

5. Executing a survey requires more than just the design of the survey instrument. Sampling can be used to target subgroups and establish quasi experiments as groups are compared to each other. We will not go into how to design samples that target and measure specific issues in the workforce. See C. C. Hoffmann and J. S. Reed, "Sex Discrimination? The XYZ Affair," *The Public Interest*, Winter 1981, as an example. There are very sophisticated methods that have been available for years, such as path analysis, which allows for the estimation of the combination of direct and indirect effects that can illuminate causation and actions to be taken. See Hubert M. Blalock Jr., *Theory Construction* (Englewood Cliffs, NJ: Prentice-Hall, 1969). Fortunately, the problems most companies face can be explained by simpler techniques. These techniques are easier to explain to the users who must act on the findings. But the researchers should appreciate the limitations of these simpler techniques and realize that what may appear straightforward can be wrong.

6. The combination of the answers to these six questions is highly correlated with departures. A measurement technique called factor analysis was used to confirm and inform the scales that we used in the analysis; see Harry H. Harman, *Modern Factor Analysis* (Chicago: University of Chicago Press, 1970). This technique measures how closely correlated a set of responses to several questions are to each other and can measure how distinct or orthogonal that set of questions is from other sets of questions. The scales presented here were all subject to that analysis.

Chapter 5

1. In this chapter, we intend only to highlight the potential value of using social network analysis as a measurement approach in organizations. For those who are looking for a more in-depth understanding of applying social network analysis to corporations, see one of the more useful books on the subject, written by two former IBM colleagues: Rob Cross and Andrew Parker, *The Hidden Power of Social Networks: Understanding How Work Really Gets Done in Organizations* (Boston: Harvard Business School Press, 2004).

2. Rob Cross, Kate Ehrlich, Ross Dawson, and John Helferich, "Managing Collaboration: Improving Team Effectiveness Through a Network Perspective," *California Management Review* 50, no. 4 (Summer 2008): 74–98.

3. Lynn Wu, Ching-Yung Lin, Sinan Aral, and Erik Brynjolfsson, "Value of Social Network—A Large Scale Analysis on Network Structure Impact to Financial Revenue of Information Technology Consultants" (working paper presented at the Winter Information Systems Conference, Salt Lake City, UT, February 2009).

4. James Surowiecki, *The Wisdom of Crowds* (New York: Doubleday, 2004), 222.

5. Bill Roberts, "HR Technology Data-Driven Human Capital Decisions," *HR Magazine* 52, no. 3 (March 1, 2007): 17–18.

Chapter 6

1. For an in-depth discussion of regression techniques, see C. C. Hoffmann and D. Quade, "Regression and Discrimination: A Case of Lack of Fit," in *Sociological Methods and Research* (Beverly Hills, CA: Sage Publications, May 1983).

2. Howard M. Taylor and Samuel Karlin, *An Introduction to Stochastic Modeling*, 3rd ed. (San Diego, CA: Academic Press, 1998); Sheldon M. Ross, *Stochastic Processes*, 2nd ed. (New York, NY: John Wiley & Sons, 1995); S. Vajda, *Mathematics of Manpower Planning* (Chichester, U.K.: John Wiley & Sons, 1978); and D. J. Bartholomew, *Stochastic Models for Social Processes*, 2nd ed. (Chichester, U.K.: Wiley, 1973).

Chapter 7

1. Boris Groysberg and Eliot Sherman, "The Royal Bank of Scotland Group: The Human Capital Strategy," Case N9-408-060 (Boston: Harvard Business School Publishing, 2008), 11.

2. For more information on the importance of focal jobs, see Eric Lesser, Denis Brousseau, and Tim Ringo, "Focal Jobs—Viewing Talent Through a Different Lens," IBM Institute for Business Value Executive Brief, 2009.

3. Groysberg and Sherman, "The Royal Bank of Scotland Group," 3.

[**ACKNOWLEDGMENTS**]

We are fortunate to have worked with clients that trusted our expertise even when the process of analysis was difficult and the outcome uncertain. Many of the cases cited in the book are the result of teamwork. The collaboration of many people at Delta Air Lines over the years and most recently Steve Dickson, senior vice president-Flight Operations, has been invaluable. Similarly, we would also like to thank Kevin Brown and Qantas Airlines; Robin Wilson and Luxottica Retail; Sandy Price, Lonnie Johnston, Melinda Tiemeyer, and Sprint; and Greig Aitken and The Royal Bank of Scotland for their time and effort. Jeff Joerres and Mara Swan of the ManpowerGroup, and Robert Bleimeister, Richard Taylor, Mary Young, and Wayne Cascio all read the early versions of the book and provided important insight.

Over the years at many companies, there are people whose help and support have been an inspiration: Randy McDonald, Mirian Graddick-Weir, Charlie Tharp, Hunter Hughes, Mary Sue Rogers, Fred Miller, Ken Sloan, David Erickson, Sandra Evers-Manly, Peter Korsten, and John Greer. We have also been fortunate to work with many gifted team members including the folks at the Mathematics Laboratory at IBM Research—Mark Squilanti, Brenda Dietrich, and Dan Connors among many. We owe a lot to Bruce Johnson, Robert Rupar, Robert Wininger, and Tom Stachura, all of whom helped to develop systematic, rigorous, and quick ways of getting at and using data. Kathleen Hoffmann and Arianna Hoffmann have given advice and help on the research and writing that is the basis for much of the insight found in this book. Over the years Sally Spetz has contributed her knowledge and expertise in job analysis and human factors reflected in this work. A great debt is owed to Krishna Namboodiri, Dana Quade, Amos Hawley, and John Reed, whose admonition that determining the critical research question is critical to selecting the correct analytical approach and that research and storytelling are not incompatible.

At Harvard Business Review Press, we would like to thank Melinda Merino for shaping our initial thoughts into a book, Ania Wieckowski for keeping our momentum going, and Tim Sullivan, Jennifer Waring, and Kevin Evers for helping us get across the finish line.

Carl C. Hoffmann has been helping companies around the world meet the challenges of formulating and implementing effective human resource strategies for more than thirty years. From 1978 until 1999, Hoffmann was CEO of a successful private consulting firm that focused on helping companies collect and analyze data to support strategic workforce decisions. When his company was purchased by PricewaterhouseCoopers, Hoffmann joined PwC as a partner. At PwC he helped develop and lead the Integrated Analytics practice for the Americas, as well as the global Workforce Analytics practice. In 2002, when IBM acquired the PwC Management Consulting Group, Hoffmann became a partner and vice president of IBM's Global Business Services group. In all of these roles, he designed and ran a number of large workforce transformation projects for multinational companies. Since retiring from IBM in 2007, Hoffmann has established a private consulting firm, Human Capital Management and Performance LLC (HCMP), which continues to work with corporate executives to make fact-based decisions that integrate workforce activities with line operations to achieve strategic goals.

Hoffmann has given presentations on public policy before U.S. House and Senate committees, and on statistics, business process redesign, and technology implementation for the American Statistical Association, the International Association for

Human Resource Information Management, and the Society for Human Resource Management. He is also the author of numerous publications, reports, and white papers dealing with human resource analysis and research methodology. He holds a PhD in sociology with a concentration in biostatistics from the University of North Carolina at Chapel Hill.

Eric Lesser is the Research Director and North American leader for the IBM Institute for Business Value. He oversees a global team responsible for driving IBM's research and thought leadership on strategic business issues.

Previously, he led IBM's Global Business Services research and thought leadership in the area of human capital management. His research and consulting have focused on a variety of issues, including workforce and talent management, collaboration, social networking and knowledge management, and the changing role of the HR organization. As a consultant, he has worked with clients across a range of industries, including the financial services, legal, technology, and government sectors.

Lesser speaks frequently on a range of human capital topics and has edited (with Laurence Prusak) *Creating Value with Knowledge: Insights from the IBM Institute for Business Value* (2003). He also edited *Knowledge and Social Capital* and co-edited *Knowledge and Communities* (2000). He has written numerous articles for publications such as the *Sloan Management Review*, the *Academy of Management Executive*, the *International Human Resources Information Management Journal*, and the *Journal of Business Strategy*. He has been quoted in numerous publications, including the *Wall Street Journal, BusinessWeek*, the *Financial Times*, and the *Chicago Tribune*, and has appeared on *Fox Business News, BBC News*, and *CBC Newsworld*.

260

Lesser received his MBA from Emory University, where he was a Robert W. Woodruff Fellow. He graduated *summa cum laude* from Brandeis University with a BA in Economics. He has also studied at the London School of Economics.

Tim Ringo has over twenty years of experience helping organizations develop engaged, high-performing workforces aligned to business objectives. He has worked with CEOs and corporate-level HR professionals in successfully implementing large-scale human resource programs that produce measurable results. He has implemented workforce solutions across an array of industries, including financial services, communications, high tech, manufacturing and transportation, and across the world—in the Americas, Europe, and many parts of Asia.

Ringo is currently a partner at London-based Maxxim Consulting. Previously he was vice president and global leader of IBM's Human Capital Management (HCM) consulting practice, where he led a team of more than fifteen hundred human capital consulting professionals around the world. He joined IBM Global Business Services in 2006 after sixteen years at Accenture, where he was an executive partner in Accenture's Human Performance Service line.

Based in London for fifteen years, he holds a Bachelor of Science in Business Administration from The Ohio State University. He also studied English Literature at Ohio State and New College, Oxford, England. He is a sought after speaker, commentator and writer on human capital topics, and the author of a number of white papers and articles.